# CURING
# PSYCHOLOGICAL
# SYMPTOMS

## Books by the Author

*The Psychoanalysis of Symptoms*

*Dictionary of Psychopathology*

*Group Psychotherapy and Personality: Intersecting Structures*

*Sleep Disorders: Insomnia and Narcolepsy*

*The 4 Steps to Peace of Mind* (Romanian edition, 2008; Japanese edition, 2011; reissued by The American Mental Health Foundation as *Curing Psychological Symptoms*, 2020)

*Love Is Not Enough: What It Takes to Make It Work*

*Greedy, Cowardly, and Weak: Hollywood's Jewish Stereotypes*

*Hollywood Movies on the Couch: A Psychoanalyst Examines 15 Famous Films*

*Haggadah: A Passover Seder for the Rest of Us*

*Personality: How It Forms* (Korean edition, 2016)

*The Discovery of God: A Psycho/Evolutionary Perspective*

*A Consilience of Natural and Social Sciences: A Memoir of Original Contributions*

*Anatomy of Delusion*

*Psychoanalysis of Evil: Perspectives on Destructive Behavior*

*There's No Handle on My Door: Stories of Patients in Mental Hospitals* (Audiobook, 2018)

*Psychotherapeutic Traction: Uncovering the Patient's* Power-theme *and* Basic-wish

## Scheduled for Release, 2020–21

*On the Nature of Nature*

*Curing Psychological Symptoms*

*The Origin of Language*

## The Ghost Trilogy

*The Making of Ghosts: A Novel*

*Ghosts of Dreams: A Novel*

*The Ghost: A Novel*


## Coauthored Books (with Anthony Burry, Ph.D.)

*Psychopathology and Differential Diagnosis: A Primer*
Volume 1. *History of Psychopathology*
Volume 2. *Diagnostic Primer*

*Handbook of Psychodiagnostic Testing: Analysis and Personality in the Psychological Report*
First edition, 1981; Second edition, 1991; Third edition, 1997; Fourth edition, 2007 (Japanese edition, 2011)


## Edited Books

*Group Cohesion: Theoretical and Clinical Perspectives*

*The Nightmare: Psychological and Biological Foundations*


## Coedited Books (with Robert Plutchik, Ph.D.)

*Emotion: Theory, Research, and Experience*
Volume 1. *Theories of Emotion*
Volume 2. *Emotions in Early Development*
Volume 3. *Biological Foundations of Emotion*
Volume 4. *The Measurement of Emotion*
Volume 5. *Emotion, Psychopathology, and Psychotherapy*

*The Emotions Profile Index: Test and Manual*, 1976

# CURING
# PSYCHOLOGICAL
# SYMPTOMS

## Henry Kellerman, Ph.D.

2020

**AMHF**

AMERICAN
MENTAL
HEALTH
FOUNDATION
BOOKS

American Mental Health Foundation Inc
128 Second Place Garden Suite
Brooklyn New York 11231-4102

Box 3
Riverdale New York 10471-0003

Originally published as *The 4 Steps to Peace of Mind:
The Simple Effective Way to Cure Our Emotional Symptoms*

Copyright © 2020 by Henry Kellerman

Printed in the United States of America

americanmentalhealthfoundation.org

Library of Congress Cataloging-in-Publication Data

Names: Kellerman, Henry, author.
Title: Curing psychological symptoms / Henry Kellerman, Ph.D.
Other titles: 4 steps to peace of mind
Description: Brooklyn, New York : American Mental Health Foundation Inc.,
2020. | Revision of: 4 steps to peace of mind. c2007.
Identifiers: LCCN 2019031251 (print) | LCCN 2019031252 (ebook) |
ISBN 9781590566046 (hardcover) | ISBN 9781590566053 (paperback) |
ISBN 9781590566060 (ebook)
Subjects: LCSH: Psychoanalysis. | Symptoms. | Psychotherapy.
Classification: LCC RC506 .K438 2020 (print) | LCC RC506 (ebook) |
DDC 616.89/17—dc23
LC record available at https://lccn.loc.gov/2019031251
LC ebook record available at https://lccn.loc.gov/2019031252

To protect privacy, all identifying information of clinical-subject
material has been changed. This includes names, places, personal history,
physical characteristics, and demographics.

*To the memory of*

*Nathan Kamen*

*Teacher—dear friend—great pathfinder*

# Contents

**Part 5**
**Summary of the Symptom Code**

# Publisher's Foreword

As this book is issued, The American Mental Health Foundation continues its growth through ten decades of philanthropic endeavors: a century of excellence in mental-health research. AMHF is dedicated to the welfare of people suffering from emotional problems, with a particular concern for at-risk youth, individuals of any age with special needs, and elders. Historically, from the post–World War II era to 2005, AMHF devoted its efforts to bettering quality of treatment, and developing more effective methods, making both available and accessible to individuals of modest incomes. Over the past fifteen years, the extended mission of AMHF lies in three areas: research, education, and publishing.

\* \* \*

*Curing Psychological Symptoms* speaks to this tripartite mission as it adds to Dr. Henry Kellerman's expansive oeuvre. In this book, written for clinicians as well as the curious general reader, Kellerman examines psychological symptoms such as phobias and compulsions, as well as illuminating *a symptom code* with respect to the four empowering factors we need to know about them. The reader is guided through these four elements related to all emotional symptoms: *the wishes, the anger, the who,* and *the to do.*

"The fantastic fact is that psychotherapists have never really had a map or an instruction manual that they all could follow so that any symptom could be unlocked and cured," Dr. Kellerman writes. "Even though psychotherapists know a great deal about the processes of psychotherapeutic treatment, the sad fact is that nowhere is there any spelled-out technique that therapists systematically use to penetrate the symptom and then cure it."

This book is far more than a technical treatise. It considers ten fascinating cases to show how Dr. Kellerman's methods have *worked* for more than half-a-century of private practice. A majority among the profiled do not require medication, some do. Rather than discussing "the cure," Dr. Kellerman employs the far-more-realistic therapeutic goal of *struggling better,* a faithful reflection of what the therapeutic process is about.

\* \* \*

Since formation in the month that Sigmund Freud was on the cover of *Time* magazine—as one of the pioneering nonprofit foundations of its kind—The American Mental Health Foundation has remained a force in research and advocacy. Its therapeutic advances and improved training methods are described in several publications: the three-part series The Search for the Future. Two of these books are available gratis on the AMHF website under the titles *The Challenge for Group Psychotherapy* (volume 1, 1974) and *The Challenge for Psychoanalysis and Psychotherapy: Solutions for the Future* (volume 2, 1999). Portions of these books are also reprinted on the AMHF website in French and German. Volume 3 (2000) is available from AMHF Books in traditional as well as low-priced e-formats: *Crucial Choices—Crucial Changes: The Resurrection of Psychotherapy.*

In addition to *Crucial Choices—Crucial Changes* by Dr. Stefan de Schill, and his related titles in English, French, and German on its website, this not-for-profit publishing program includes four classic books (two reissued, two posthumous) by Erich Fromm; five additional by Dr. Kellerman on group psychotherapy, personality formation, and the lives of patients in mental hospitals; nine by Dr. Raymond B. Flannery Jr., for professionals in several areas as well as general readers, on violence and stress at the breaking point (PTSD), the latest being *Coping with Anxiety in an Age of Terrorism* (2017); one on the psychological stresses faced by women executives, authored by Drs. Joanne H. Gavin, James Campbell Quick, and David J. Gavin; and, collaborating with Astor Services for Children & Families, *Early Identification, Palliative Care, and Prevention of Psychotic Disorders in Children and Youth,* the culmination of a rigorous two-year AMHF study in 2016.

Several other books are presently scheduled into 2021: *The Origin of Language* and *Preventing Youth Violence before It Begins.*

\* \* \*

The costs of promoting research, organizing seminars and webinars, and disseminating the findings in fulfillment of the mission of The American Mental Health Foundation, are high. All gifts, made via PayPal (this foundation is proud to be recognized by the PayPal Charitable Giving Fund) on the foundation website or posted to the address listed on the copyright page of this book, constitute a meaningful contribution to the public good. If your commitment is deeper, consider partnering with AMHF in the form of a legacy bequest, so that the foundation can continue to serve society for another century. We thank you for your interest in the present book as well as for helping AMHF build a more compassionate society. Please discover for yourself the work of The American Mental Health Foundation in greater detail on its website.

americanmentalhealthfoundation.org

# Introduction

---

"This anxiety is driving me crazy," a woman says. A man says, "I can't stop counting everything I do—count, count, count—see, I said it three times!" Crying, another woman exclaimed, "I'm always crying—at the slightest thing—damn it!" Answering for her husband, still another woman said, "He can't face going to any social thing: parties, a wedding, anything." Then there was the man who reported that every night before he could go to sleep, he would need to check the locks on his front door, "over and over," he said. How about this man who maintains that "Things pop into my head and sometimes they scare me, like I might do something wrong to someone." While holding a handkerchief over his mouth, another man says, "I don't touch doorknobs or light switches or anything that's loaded with germs."

All of these people are talking about their *psychological symptoms*. Migraine headaches, fear of heights, fear of open spaces, scary thoughts that you can't shake, obsessions, ritual behaviors, compulsions, as well as innumerable others.

Have you ever had any? Not to worry. Actually, all people have such symptoms at one time or another.

When I first trained as a psychologist and then as a psychoanalyst, these were some of the problems that interested me. So, in the past fifty-plus years, I have worked with people in clinics and hospitals, as well as in private practice, and have had the chance to see all kinds of symptoms up close. In most cases, when I ask them, patients would usually say that it was their main *relationship* (or not having one) that bothered them. Yet, what they would always, *always* say when it came to the cure, was that it was their *symptom* that they wanted to cure.

### What Is an Emotional/Psychological Symptom?

When people sense they are having an experience that they cannot control, it's a good bet that they are already in touch with the eerie presence of a symptom. An emotional/psychological symptom, therefore, is some experience that you feel is really out of your control. Basically, you just can't control it. Your symptom controls you, and on top of it all there's not much that you could do about it. The symptom will dominate you. It is at such times that you know that some inner force—different from and greater than the force of your conscious mind—is present. If you have ever had such an experience then you know it feels strange, it is definitely inconvenient, and a lot of the time it is downright embarrassing.

### Does Anyone Know How to Cure a Psychological Symptom?

Over the years, I slowly began to tease out the elements of *the symptom*—to see inside—into how a psychological symptom works, how it develops, and how curing it might then be accomplished. The fantastic fact is that psychotherapists have never really had a map or an instruction manual that they all could follow so that any symptom could be unlocked and cured. Even though psychotherapists know a great deal about the processes of psychotherapeutic treatment, the sad fact is that nowhere is there any spelled-out technique that therapists systematically use to penetrate the symptom and then cure it. The symptom cannot just be wished away, and it cannot be reasoned with—it won't listen! To cure the symptom, you need to know its code, what it is made of. Even Freud, who tells a lot about symptoms, never set forth the equation, the formula, *the basic code of the symptom,* so that we would know how to reach in and cure it.

### What this Book Aims to Do

Exactly such a formula—*a symptom code* as I call it—is set forth here. When used, this formula can unfold, penetrate, and cure the symptom. In other words, it is my aim that a person use this book to understand, alleviate, and even cure his or her own symptom and thereby gain a greater measure of peace of mind. In some cases, a combination of the symptom code and medication is needed to improve or alleviate a symptom.

In part 1 I describe the four points of the symptom code, which are outlined below on page 20.

In part 2, I present a series of symptoms and show how the symptom code is used to cure the problem. In part 3, I describe what the symptom really means so that you have a greater understanding of what you are experiencing. In part 4, I present a series

---

**THE FOUR POINTS OF THE SYMPTOM CODE**

(1) You have *a wish* but you may not realize its presence.

(2) You are *angry,* although you may not be aware of it.

(3) You are angry at someone specific: *a who.*

(4) You need *to do* something about POINT I: *the wish.*

---

of symptoms that resist cure through the use of the symptom code and show why medication is needed in these instances to help provide a cure. I summarize the symptom code in part 5.

When you finally see or understand the answer to each of the four points outlined, you recognize that you have *a wish,* that you are *angry* at a specific person *(a who),* and that you need *to do* something about it. Then you will be well on your way to curing your symptom.

Let's begin.

# PART ONE

# The Key to Unlocking the Symptom

*The One, Two, Three, and Four
of Symptom-cure*

# CHAPTER ONE

# Point One Is *the Wish*

It all starts with wishes. Almost all things are wishes. We are wish-soaked creatures. What this means is that people have all kinds of wishes, all the time. On top of that, we usually make no distinction between big wishes and little wishes. They're all big to us. We want what we want when we want it! Basically, the wish comes out of what is known as *the pleasure principle.* This means that people want to feel good, satisfied, content, gratified, and pleasured all the time. People want to be free of unpleasant feelings. The problem is that life is constructed in such a way that our wishes usually are not met. Or if they are met, they are not exactly how we would have wanted them met. Or if they are met as we wanted, then it is frequently the case that they are not met exactly when we wanted them. Or if our wishes are met precisely when we wanted them, it is typically not to the fullest measure.

The point is that most of the time we need things, want things, pray for things, wish for things—*needing, wanting, praying, wishing*—all more or less the same. But then we usually don't get the wish. What happens when we don't get the wish? It is simple: When we don't get our wish we feel frustrated, experience a loss of power, and our tension-level rises.

Then what happens? We look for ways to feel better. We usually do this searching and looking to feel better in an automatic—an unconscious—way. It is our attempt to feel better and not to feel frustrated. We don't like to be disempowered. That is to say, we don't want to be left hanging.

This frustration business is interesting since *everyone* in the world has the same reaction to frustration. Not getting what we want and feeling frustrated because of it, or uncomfortable because of it, or upset because of it, creates a feeling of helplessness in every single person. What does helplessness mean? It means that we feel left without power. When a person is frustrated because a wish is blocked then he or she feels helpless or disempowered.

Let's take an example. You are rushing for a bus or train. You see it and you run, but it is iffy as to whether you can make it. The wish to make the bus or train is urgent. You feel that you have got to make it. And you are about to make it, running, running. As you approach the door, it suddenly closes and the vehicle begins to pull away. You are left standing there, exhausted. You're breathing hard from all that running. Now you're left at the empty bus depot or train station with packages that you've been lugging, knowing that the next bus or train will be arriving twenty minutes later (if on time), and that you will now be late for wherever it was that you were going or, fundamentally, that it would take you a lot longer to get home.

Do you feel good or powerful because your wish to catch that train was dashed? Of course not. On the contrary, you feel frustrated, powerless—*disempowered.* That is the magic word. You don't get your wish. You feel disempowered.

So far, we have *the wish, the blocking of the wish, the frustration* because of not getting the wish satisfied and the inevitable feeling that always results from this blocked wish: the feeling of powerlessness or disempowerment.

### *Things to Keep in Mind about* Wishes

*Wishes are what we want.* Wishes range from the silliest to the most serious. We need to remember that wishes are not heavily governed by the laws of logic or society. Rather they are based on our needs, attitudes, and feelings. Wishes usually concern getting things or achieving things. We wish for love, for someone's health, for someone's death. We wish to be praised. We wish for overall good tidings toward others, for overall bad tidings toward others. We wish for comforts, security, happiness, advantages, triumphs, companionship, and victories both large and small.

Now I need to mention why some symptoms relieve tension and emotional discomfort whereas other symptoms make the tension and discomfort worse. The issue is that it all relates to *wishes.* In fact, of all the symptoms presented in this book, you will see that some symptoms take the tension away whereas others make the tension worse. The question is *Why?* The answer rests in the nature of any person's wish: that is, it rests with the direction of the wish. To put it simply: If your wish is a direct one, that is, the wish is *to have* something, then the plain fact is that the symptom will relieve tension. On the other hand, if the wish is indirect, or a wish *to avoid* something, then the opposite will happen: The symptom will increase tension.

Regarding all the symptoms I present in this book, each one will be identified as containing either a wish to have something or a wish to avoid something.

Remember, we are covering the four points of the symptom code. This was Point One: *the wish*.

# CHAPTER TWO

# Point Two Is *the Anger*

If you feel a sense of disempowerment in response to *a blocked wish,* whether or not you are consciously aware of it, you will, at that moment, feel angry. What this means is that every person, on any continent, and in any corner of that continent, in any culture, regardless of religion or creed or race, will always, without fail and without exception, be angry at such feelings of disempowerment. This is a hard-core emotional/psychological law.

This law has it that anger is the natural biological, emotional, and psychological reflex to such a sense of disempowerment. You feel disempowered, and as I have said, no matter who you are or where you are, you will then feel angry. You may not always know it, or be conscious of the anger, or even in your wildest dreams think that you are angry. Nevertheless you will, in fact, be angry. Many people, even most of us, are usually not consciously aware that (a) we're feeling disempowered and (b) that we're angry in reaction to this disempowerment.

What we do know is that we are uncomfortable about something. We know that we are tense, but we are not sure that it is a sense of disempowerment and its partner, anger, which is making us uncomfortable. We are not even aware that it is anger itself that we're feeling as a result of such frustration or powerlessness or disempowerment. But we know something is wrong so we call it *being upset* or *distracted* or *tense,* or as feeling a certain kind of *anxiety;* or we use any number of other descriptions to stand in as anger, such as *annoyed* or *inconvenienced* or *impatient* or even *bored.*

What is the reason for our avoidance of knowing that we are angry when we feel disempowered? Why, in the first place, is it that anger is the natural emotional reflex to feelings of helplessness or disempowerment?

### *The Need for* Reempowerment

When we are disempowered the key is that we need to become *reempowered.* No one wants to remain in a state of disempowerment: not for a moment. The fact is that, often, when one is disempowered there is frequently no other way to become reempowered, except to get angry.

Anger is a very strong emotion and it has a powerful personality. Let's look at the personality profile of anger (page 29).

If you have an aggressive drive, if you feel that you need to be expansive, if you experience the potential to explode, and if within you there is a tendency to attack and, along with these character-

---

**THE PERSONALITY OF ANGER**

Anger has an aggressive drive. It is inborn.

Anger is expansive. It wants to get bigger.

Anger has explosive potential. It wants to burst out.

Anger has an attack inclination. It wants to attack.

Anger has a confrontational inclination. It wants to get tough.

Anger has an entitled frame of mind. It feels it has the right to get tough.

Anger sees itself as an empowerment. It eliminates feelings of helplessness.

---

istics, you feel entitled to confront others, then it becomes clearer that all of these tendencies would help any person transform his or her feelings of helplessness or disempowerment into feelings of control or power.

In this sense, when one is feeling helpless or disempowered and there is no way to rectify the helplessness or disempowerment, then it is no wonder that the emotion of anger comes into play. As I have said, however, the individual usually doesn't realize that the anger even exists. Rather, the anger becomes suppressed or repressed: pushed into the unconscious mind. The anger becomes repressed because *the who,* the person you are angry with, is usually the one person that you feel you can't afford to challenge. For instance, it may be necessary to suppress or repress anger at your boss or some other authority figure who, if you were to challenge him or her, could make life difficult for you. Instead of expressing anger, or instead of even knowing that anger exists, therefore, people often repress it: push the anger deep down into the unconscious mind and out of awareness.

But that's not the end of the story since anger is the powerful emotion—arguably the most powerful of any of the emotions—and if suppressed or repressed, the anger will push back, push from below, radiating into what we then call a state of *anxiety* or *upset* or *stress.*

We could say that in cases in which the anger does reach our consciousness and is, in fact, directly expressed toward *the who*—the person toward whom it was originally intended—then the likelihood of an emotional/psychological symptom appearing is zero! If you know *the who,* and the anger is conscious, then you will not have a symptom.

It's important—actually essential—to be aware that there is, in fact, a specific person toward whom you are angry: *the who.*

| OBVIOUS CODE WORDS FOR ANGER | |
| --- | --- |
| Rage | Quarrelsomeness |
| Fury | Loathing |
| Resentment | Contemptuousness |
| Irritability | Hatefulness |

The reason this is essential is that if you could identify *the who* toward whom you direct your anger, then you would not develop a symptom. However, if you do have a symptom then it would be a sure thing that you are harboring anger in your unconscious mind about which you are not aware, and that some specific person is the target of this anger. In such a case, wherein the anger is out of your awareness, you will additionally not even be conscious that *a who* exists.

This leads to Point Three—*the who*—which I discuss in the next chapter.

| LESS-OBVIOUS CODE WORDS FOR ANGER | |
|---|---|
| Annoyed | Sullen |
| Discontented | Bored |
| Disconcerted | Suspicious |
| Upset | Stressed |
| Anxious | Tense |
| Inconvenienced | Impatient |

# CHAPTER THREE

# Point Three Is *the Who*

It is only when the anger is pushed down into your unconscious mind and out of awareness that trouble begins. A hard-core psychological law reveals *when anger is repressed a symptom must appear.* More specifically, when anger is repressed toward a specific person, *a who,* and pushed down into your unconscious mind, that is when you will get a symptom.

Again, it must be remembered that your *wish* (Point One) starts it. When the wish is thwarted, you feel helpless and disempowered. You challenge this helplessness or disempowerment by becoming *angry* (Point Two) at the person (Point Three) who blocks the wish. And it is always a person, never a thing, which will be *the who.*

## *Who Are the Who's?*

*The who's* are the personal cast of characters of your life. It is always important to know who it is that is responsible for blocking your wish. This is the first job that you have to do. You must know who it is that makes you feel helpless, that has turned you down, rejected you, refused you something, or blocked the path to your goal—your *wish*.

At first glance, this can seem like a hard problem to solve. Doesn't everybody have scads of people in their lives? How does one narrow it down to see who the culprit is—the responsible *who?*

## *The Usual Suspects*

The good news is that the problem is far less complicated than it seems. The fact is that each one of us really has fewer than six or seven significant people that might be "our culprit": our targeted *who.* In order to get the correct *who,* we need to identify who that might be. For this job we need to round up the usual suspects.

Of the usual suspects—those that can affect us, scare us, or make us angry—*the who* will be that person responsible for us not getting what we want (not getting what we wish for). Thus, *the who* is the person that prevents us from getting our wish.

## *Let's Round Them Up*

When we try to think of just who *the who* might be, we can become overwhelmed. After all, one knows so many people.

There are probably forty, fifty, or even a hundred people in every life.

No, that's wrong. Those people, or suspects, who can affect us enough to cause the kind of emotional stress and distress that leads to the appearance of some psychological symptom, are really members of an exclusive club. How many members are in this club? The answer is anywhere from five, six, seven up to ten. That's about it. Ten is even high. These few members of your *Who Club* can include your spouse, your child, one of your parents, one of your siblings, another one of your relatives, and even your employer, a particular coworker, a close friend, or even some other accidental person.

| OUR USUAL SUSPECTS | |
| --- | --- |
| A spouse | A fiancé |
| A parent | A child |
| A sibling | An employer |
| A friend | A coworker |
| A relative | A business associate |

When you are experiencing a symptom and looking for *the who,* you need to do a mental roundup of about five or six or seven people in order to see which of them might be the culprit, the one that caused your feelings of dissatisfaction or hurt; that scared you; or made you feel stupid, helpless, humiliated; or who said *No* to you and made you feel helpless, disempowered, and then angry.

As pointed out, sometimes it is hard to realize that you are, in fact, angry. But if you are experiencing a symptom, you can be

> **BEST BET**
>
> The person with whom you are closest.
>
> The person who has power over you.
>
> The person with whom you've shared an important event.
>
> The person you love.
>
> The person you hate.
>
> The accidental person with whom you've had some random encounter.

sure that the anger is definitely there: underneath. Even if you don't feel the anger, try to see if you have a feeling of dissatisfaction. The feeling of dissatisfaction is usually a good roadmap to follow. It will lead you to your destination—the feeling of anger and the feeling of anger toward a specific person—*the who.*

Now, we still have one more point to cover in our dissection of the symptom code. Point One was a consideration of *the wish.* Point Two was an analysis of the issue of *anger,* and Point Three covered the concept of anger toward a specific person: *the who.* Our final Point Four concerns *what to do* with respect to the original wish.

# CHAPTER FOUR

# Point Four Is *to Do*

If you have symptoms and know what your *wish* was, who was *the who* blocking your wish, and you are also able to identify the feeling of dissatisfaction or *anger* that is surely lurking, perhaps even boiling within you, there is a good chance that you will, in fact, be able to conquer the symptom.

Thus, to know the three components or points of the symptom code *(the wish, the anger,* and *the who)* will definitely challenge the strength of the symptom and, most often, cause the symptom to lose the effective grip it had on you and on your personality. To make sure the symptom is cured however, a *to-do* job will be a further deathblow to the symptom.

This "doing" thing will be related to the original wish that was blocked in the first place. Examples include such things as completing a job that was originally blocked, asking someone something that you couldn't originally ask, and the like. The point is to accomplish something or to work on something that is related in a fashion to the blocked wish.

### *The Line*

The *to-do* thing is never something that you do in your mind. In your mind you are, so to speak, *behind the line.* If we imagine a line, we can see that when we exist behind it we are in a fantasy, or in a thinking mode, or even in a state of withdrawal. *Behind the line* is *a not-doing-place.* It is only when we are in front of *the line* that we exist in a doing-place. In this sense, *the to-do* activity, by definition, is an *in-front-of-the- line* activity, in a doing-place.

This is where the *to do* has to take place: in front of *the line,* The *to do* must be proactive and, as stated, must be related to the original wish, and, also usually, related to *the who* that was involved in blocking the original wish. Therefore, the *to-do* thing is usually the attempt to try to complete something, or the working on the something that you were prevented from doing or working on in the first place.

It is important for you to know that the *to do* does not depend on your actual full completion of the problem and then gaining the something you wanted in the first place: the something you wished for. The importance of the *to do* refers rather to some attempt to approach the original problem, even if it's only a little step that reaches into the dilemma.

Now, after seeing each of the four points of the symptom code, we can look at some cases wherein the symptom code was used.

# PART TWO

# Using the Symptom Code with Actual Symptoms

*These are symptoms that respond to the symptom code without the use of any medications.*

# CHAPTER FIVE

# A Case of Compulsion

## *Bottles under the Bed*

In order to relieve "the funny feelings" he gets in his stomach, an eleven-year-old boy compulsively begins putting bottles under his bed.

### *What Happened*

Josh suddenly started experiencing what he called "funny" or "bad feelings" in his stomach. He said he knew, almost automatically, that if he put bottles under the bed the funny feelings would disappear. That's just what he did. Whenever he had the funny feelings, he would gather some bottles that were in the house and place them under the bed. At that point the funny or bad feelings would immediately disappear. "It was like magic," he said.

## Using the Symptom Code

Based on the symptom code of *one* (the wish), *two* (the anger), and *three* (the who), we would guess that Josh

(1)   had some wish blocked
(2)   got angry about it
(3)   and didn't realize that he was angry at someone in particular: *a who.*

Josh was able to remember that several months earlier, about the time he began experiencing his 'funny feelings" symptom, his parents had, as he characterized it, "a screaming fight." It was the first time that he had ever seen them fight like this, and the intensity of the fight scared him. He even became more upset when, in the throes of this argument, his father threatened to divorce his mother.

Josh was an only child, and it was impossible for him to contemplate this kind of catastrophic fracture of his family. Since family was the most-important thing in the world to him, and since he took his father's threat to divorce his mother so seriously, it appeared that this was the pivotal event that triggered his bottles' symptom, especially since it was a day or two later that he started experiencing "the funny feelings" in his stomach.

But at that point in his life something else that was funny, or strangely different, also started happening to him. *Other things* started happening to him. It was as if he started a new life, a different one.

### *Josh's Story Surrounding the Symptom of the Bottles*

Josh was in middle school, in the eighth grade. About the same time that the funny-feeling stomach started, each day after school when he got home he began telling his mother that he was going to the library to study or to do some library work for school. Off he went, carrying some books. Yet instead of heading to the library, Josh would go to the movies. This need to go to the movies would begin to get a hold on him whenever school let out for the day.

Josh knew what it meant. He could feel it. He felt it right away. All those movies were an escape from his homework. That's what it felt like. But that is what was funny, since he was always prepared for school. But not anymore. On top of that, when he was in school his teachers began noticing that he was daydreaming: looking toward the window and staring. One of his good teachers called home and told Josh's mother that he was not as interested in his work as he had been and that she was concerned. When his mother asked him about it, Josh straightforwardly replied, *I'm just not that interested in all that stuff. It's got nothing to do with me. You know, French and math.*

Additionally, Josh stopped seeing his friends. Ricky, Josh's best friend, didn't get his phone calls returned as quickly as they ordinarily would.

What was it that was distracting Josh, absorbing all of his focus and thinking? What was the change all about, and how did it figure into his funny-feeling stomach? Or did it?

After the movies and when Josh finally arrived home, it would be dinnertime. But he was never really that hungry since, when in the movie house, he would buy ice cream and potato chips, and tranquilize himself with these scrumptious treats. That was one of his favorite things to do; that is, sit in the movie theater, alone, watch the movie in the dark while scooping some ice cream from the cup with each little potato chip. Of course, by the time he wandered home his appetite was compromised. Besides that, he would always find a different route home, so that he would wind up roaming through neighborhoods that were strange to him.

Then as soon as he got home, he would gradually notice that he needed to put bottles under the bed. That's how it went, day in and day out: no school interest, movies instead of homework, uncovering new ways by which to return home, avoiding friendships, no interest in dinner, and then bottles under the bed. Surprisingly, Josh really thought he understood it all.

When describing all of this to me, he said that he had been feeling "down" for some time, and so he just didn't feel like going to school. For him, the movies meant that he could feel the same way the hero felt: "strong, and like things worked out for him." As far as avoiding his friends, especially Ricky, Josh said that he knew he couldn't share any secrets with him anymore since all of their secrets were silly anyway. The different routes he took to get home were somewhat of a mystery to him, although he stated, "When I'm in these different places that I don't know, it feels like I feel." As far as the bottles under the bed, this stumped him.

And that's where we begin.

### *Describing the Symptom*

Josh described the bottles' symptom in detail. When asked which bed did he put the bottles under, he indicated that it was his parents' bed.

To the question: "Which side of their bed did you place the bottles?"

He answered: Only under my father's side."

Then to the question: "What kind of bottles were they?"

He answered: "Medicine bottles, even Band-Aid boxes, and even empty medicine bottles—always something abut medicine and getting better when you're sick."

### *The Symptom Code*

The symptom code could now be applied to each element of Josh's story.

One: *The wish* that was threatened concerned wanting his family to stay intact. This was a direct wish so that the symptom of putting bottles under the bed relieved his tension.

Two: The fact that Josh thought his family would not remain intact made him quite angry, even though consciously he only felt afraid.

Three: The person, *the who,* toward whom he felt angry, was apparently his father. The bottles only went under his father's side of the bed.

Josh's ingenious system could now be understood.

### *The Meaning of the Symptom*

First of all, the funny or bad feeling in his stomach was really anger toward his father that Josh pushed away from his conscious mind. The bottles under the bed cured his funny-feeling stomach since the bottles contained medicine, whether real or imagined. When Josh put medicine (even Band-Aids) under his father's side of the bed, his bad or funny feelings would disappear since, in Josh's unconscious mind, this medicine would waft through the mattress and then somehow be absorbed by his father, thereby curing his father of not loving the mother. Thus, his father would indeed love his wife, and no divorce would be needed.

Josh would do this "curing" over and over. The funny or bad feelings would come, and Josh would cure them, always the same way, by putting bottles under the bed.

With this incredible symptom of his, Josh was preserving his parents' marriage and gratifying his basic wish that the family remain together. Josh's positive wish to cure his father also produced a symptom that relieved his tension.

In addition, all of his strange new activities that accompanied his bottles' symptom also cleared up. First, he couldn't take school seriously, since how could he concentrate on objective material such as math or a foreign language when all one is concerned about is one's personal life? Therefore, in class, when the teacher would point out that he was staring out the window, it would surprise him, and he would realize it was true: He was staring out of the window. To boot, he could not remember what it was that he was thinking about during staring episodes. Of course, the answer was that he was gripped by the tension concerning his parents, and that's all he could think about even though he couldn't remember what it was that he was thinking.

Second, films were an escape from his anxiety; and he was right about the potato chips and ice cream, too: They soothed him, so it was as if he were self-medicating. Not only was his appetite compromised by this little movie repast, but whenever he was home his bad feelings got so intense that his appetite was affected. When he was that sad, he could not really eat.

As far as Ricky was concerned, the problem was that Josh was embarrassed to tell anyone his deepest, darkest secret about his fractured family life; and the secret was so deep that he himself didn't quite know it, even though he realized that something was wrong.

Finally, his taking different routes home from the theater and traversing neighborhoods that he did not know meant that he was playing out feelings of being alien and different, an episode that passed. But, obviously for Josh, it didn't just pass. What it did was translate into a bottles-under-the-bed symptom, carrying with it a host of new behaviors for him. Thankfully, we got to the problem in time.

### To Do: *In Front of* the Line

Finally, with respect to symptom-code Point Four, *the to do*, a request was made to have a family session in which Josh could talk it over with his parents. That was "an in front of *the line*" doing thing. The family session took place. His father assured Josh that he, in fact, loved Josh's mother. As Josh's father put it, the comment about divorce during that terrible argument was nothing more than "Just one of those things: blowing off steam." And that was that! Josh looked at this father, looked at his mother, and they looked back at him, as though to say, *OK? See? It's true. Everything's OK. We love each other, we love you, and we will never divorce! We're a family!* Of course, they were sincere and definite about it, and Josh could see this.

*The one, two, three* of symptom-cure required knowing:

(1)   what *the wish* was
(2)   that Josh was *angry*
(3)   and that the person—*the who*—toward whom he was angry, was his father.

The fourth point of the symptom code, *the to do*, in this case was to convene a family session and talk it over, after which Josh's symptom was just a memory.

# CHAPTER SIX

# A Case of an Intrusive Thought

### *Fear of Strangling Someone*

When alone with his girlfriend, a man panics because he suddenly begins to think of strangling her.

### *What Happened?*

Ted, a single man in his fifties, was out on a date. The evening consisted of dinner and a movie, and when they ended up at the woman's apartment they engaged in some light-amorous activity. Ted's date was apparently quite loquacious. As he explained to me, "She talked a blue streak all night."

At one point when they were in bed, Ted was suddenly gripped by the thought that he wanted to strangle her. This is called *an intrusive thought,* one that seems to appear out of the clear-blue sky and cannot be voluntarily put out of one's mind. This kind of thought then becomes obsessive.

No matter how he tried, it was a thought Ted couldn't shake. He was startled by it, especially since he had also experienced the same kind of thought on a previous date with another woman. This earlier experience was for a split second, and he thought no more about it. What startled him on this date was having the thought again, even though he was with a different woman. Further, the more he tried to erase "the strangling thought," the less he was able to. He then became frightened—alarmed, actually—excused himself, and fled.

### Using the Symptom Code

Based on the symptom code of *one (the wish)*, *two (the anger)*, and *three (the who)*, we would guess that Ted:

(1)  had his wish blocked
(2)  got angry about it
(3)  and didn't realize he was angry at someone in particular: *a who.*

Ted was never able to have a relationship because, as he said, he would "get bored with everyone." He was a successful businessman but always in arguments with employees and clients. However, he did well for those same people, largely because he was efficient and generous, especially in doling out bonuses.

But he was an impatient person and, along with his impatience, he was insensitive to others. In contrast, he wanted everyone else to be patient, tolerant, and sensitive to *his* needs. He said that he loved it when others would focus on him and also appreciated opportunities to talk about himself. He was quite interested in his appearance and would spend undue amounts of time in front of any mirror, checking to see whether he was looking as good as he wanted to.

### Ted's Story Surrounding the Strangling Symptom

Ted was sexually obsessed. He was always thinking about sexual things that, as he explained, "Would turn me on." As a matter of fact, he would be happiest when looking for sexual things to think about that would, indeed, turn him on. The looking for such things meant doing a lot of fantasizing and thinking, choosing certain women to think about who excited him. As far as he was concerned, his main problem was then finding a safe place to masturbate after he was turned on. This search for such places was ongoing every day of the week.

At night, he would masturbate in bed, and that would satisfy the kind of activity required to get some sleep. It was his daytime activities that were problematic, but he hit on something that he felt most hadn't even thought about. You see, Ted's business took him out of the office each day for meetings with clients and potential clients. He was a stationery distributor, all kinds of stationery supplies (staplers, paper, clips, pens). It was his occupation. His private preoccupation was finding public places that had bathrooms. He needed these places during the day because, when he would deliberately try to excite himself with sexual fantasies, he would want, and need, to masturbate. The question was: Where to do it?

Here was his brainstorm: *hotels.* In Manhattan there are countless hotels, especially in midtown. Every sizable hotel has a restroom in its lobby. Wherever he was in Manhattan he would find a hotel, locate the bathroom, and masturbate in one of the stalls. When finished, he'd go on his way to the next meeting.

This sort of activity was happening all of his adult life for the past twenty-five years. Did such activity affect his life generally and his dating activity specifically? The answer is a resounding *yes.* It kept him single since he was constantly gratifying himself and thus he didn't have the motivation really to connect with anyone in a significant way. That is, his compulsive masturbation was really a substitute for a relationship, and it kept Ted single for all his adult life.

The masturbation was a relationship of self to self. This man was essentially in love with his penis, meaning essentially he was in love with himself. Of course, he always dated. But these girlfriends really constituted affairs that he was having outside his primary relationship, and this primary relationship was with himself; or, rather, his penis.

The most-immediate question, however, was: Did this symptom of his masturbation connect in any way to his symptom of the strangling fear? The upshot is that he had two symptoms. The acute one was his strangling fear. The chronic one was his compulsive masturbation. It was pretty clear that the acute-strangling fear would be the easier to cure. The masturbation symptom, however, would probably require some extensive-therapy work.

### Describing the Symptom

Ted said when his date would talk about him he felt good, and that he tolerated the conversation well. The problem for him was when his date would talk about everything except him. Then he would become bored, impatient, and uninvolved. Usually, after such a date, he would mimic those moments when the woman in question was talking about anything except him by repeating to himself, *talk, talk, talk!*

The bottom line was if he were the one that didn't leave the relationship, then his partner would. His partner inevitably figured out that he simply could not, or would not, talk about anything except himself.

### The Symptom Code

Ted's symptom can now be unfolded by the symptom code:

One: *The wish* was for his date to stop talking about others. This was an indirect wish so that the symptom of the intrusive thought of strangling her frightened him, thus increasing his tension.

Two: Feeling deprived of his ego-gratification, that he wasn't being focused on, made him angry. But he didn't realize it.

Three: The person toward whom he was angry, *the who*, was his date.

Now, Ted's symptom can be more easily understood.

### *Meaning of the Symptom*

First of all, the thought of strangling his date did not literally mean that he wanted to end her life, even though that particular thought actually did panic him. What the intrusive-strangling thought signified was that he was simply angry at her. She wasn't talking about him, and this was making him impatient—a symptom for anger—that he didn't recognize. He did recognize the impatience but not the anger. Again, *talk, talk, talk!* "She wouldn't talk about *me.*"

Thus, Ted's symptom is really his basic wish, gratified, even though it is gratified in this neurotic way. That is, thinking of strangling the woman is equal to shutting her up. This means that at least the noise she was making (talking about others, which he considered to be noise), would go away so that the possibility of the focus shifting to him would increase. This is all it means. He was never in danger of strangling her, and the date was never in danger of being strangled. *Talk about me, stupid,* is what he really wanted to say.

If he had said it, he never would have had the strangling symptom.

### To Do—*in Front of* the Line

Point four, *the to do,* was for him to continue to realize that he was always trying to have someone focus on him, and that he needed to keep in mind that he was getting angry whenever this was not the case.

*The one, two, three* of symptom-cure required knowing:

(1)  what the wish was
(2)  that he was *angry*
(3)  and that the person—*the who*—toward which Ted was angry was his date.

The point here was for him to be involved in *a doing thing* that would satisfy the fourth condition of being in *a doing place:* that is, in front of *the line*. Even talking to someone about his need to focus solely on himself qualifies as *a to do*, an *in-front-of-the-line* achievement.

Once Ted realized all this, his strangling thought vanished; but his compulsive masturbation prevailed. Ted wanted to know about it. Why was he always, all his life, "so sexed-up" as he put it. The answer is that it was all about his need to aggrandize himself: to make himself bigger, better, stronger, handsomer, greater, and, finally, both heroic and generous.

All of his masturbatory fantasies—all the sex scenarios he thought of—were all about him in a position of power. They were never violent. The main story line of the fantasies had to do with the woman needing him, wanting him, beseeching him, and then needing to see his penis, which he maintained was his pride and joy, *because it's big, real big!* The deal for him was when, in his fantasy, the woman would plead to see it and then when he generously permitted her "to go get it"; she, in a moment of loss of control, would thankfully grip it in both hands. When the woman gripped his penis that way, in his fantasy, he would invariably climax.

When I told him that a case could be made that his fantasy of her grip on his penis was the equivalent to his fantasy of his grip on his date's neck—the strangling thought that frightened him so—he gasped. "Oh my God! I see what you mean. *But what does it mean?*"

What it means is that his fantasy of strangling by gripping her neck was his attempt to get her to talk only about him. At the same time, it was an attempt to re-create a gripping of something phallic, which probably represented his wish for her to talk about him so that his anger toward her could be transformed into a loving, even sexual moment, since she would be talking only about him. Her talking about him, in reality, would be the same as his fantasy in which the woman needs him desperately.

Of course, his desperation concerned his relentless need to be aggrandized: to be great.

# CHAPTER SEVEN

# A Case of Morbid Preoccupation

*Gazing at Corpses*

A physician needs to gaze at corpses, and he cannot stop the impulse to do so.

### *What Happened*

Dennis, a staff physician at a hospital, began having urges to gaze at corpses. He said that it felt as if he "wanted to look at dead bodies." When he ended his duties for the day, he would visit the pathology-department lab. There, he would look at the bodies in their various stages of dissection.

At first Dennis said, *it was just an idea.* Then, he said that his urge to look at the bodies was "like a visit." Finally, however, he admitted that to do this "was really strange."

He was right. The problem was a recurring or persistent idea in his mind, an obsession, followed by an action (his behavior), which was compulsive; that is, he would think about looking at the dead bodies and then actually go and gaze at them.

"I felt as if I were possessed, kind of like the possession you might need an exorcism for," is how he put it. He also said that whenever he visited the bodies, the tension he felt would vanish. He explained, "I liked the environment of the lab. It gave me a good feeling." In contrast, he believed that not visiting the lab when he had the urge to do so would increase his tension, and then he would feel agitated and deprived.

Dennis's wife became concerned when she noticed that he was becoming emotionally detached. She told Dennis that he was gazing into space a lot, and that he wasn't talking to her much. When she asked him what he was thinking, he would deny that anything was wrong. When she persisted, he confessed that he did know what he was thinking about: It was about looking at the dead in the hospital lab!

Dennis said that he was keeping this from her since the whole thing was most strange, even to him. His wife then thought it was a sign that he was overworked at the hospital. *No,* he said. Then, he countered with a different story. What he told her was that he had discovered that his chief of service at work had selected him to be on staff only because another doctor refused the position. He said he then realized that the insignificant assignments he was getting were based upon the chief's poor opinion of him. He said he realized, "(a) he didn't like me or didn't respect me and (b) he was discriminating against me by giving me these unimportant assignments."

Thus, the upshot was that rather than feeling overworked, Dennis felt underworked and, more importantly, undervalued.

### Using the Symptom Code

Based on our symptom code of *one (the wish)*, *two (the anger)*, and *three (the who)*, we would guess that Dennis:

(1) had his *wish* blocked

(2) got *angry* about it

(3) and didn't realize that he was angry at someone in particular: *a who*.

Of course, knowing who *the who* was is particularly important here. Although Dennis's wife, as the person closest to him, would have been a chief suspect, he knew that he was not angry at her. The person he was really angry with but couldn't face, or be fully conscious of, was his departmental chief. As it turned out, he was the best suspect.

The more Dennis described his feelings about the chief, the more certain it became that this individual was really the anger-culprit: *the who*. In describing his reactions to the chief, the physician said that he felt awkward in his chief's presence. He felt shy, withdrawn, and unnatural. He felt the chief didn't respect, trust, or even like him.

### Dennis's Story Surrounding the Symptom of Gazing at Corpses

An interesting passing comment made by the physician related to his sense of tranquility when describing the calm he felt when he was in the lab staring at these corpses. Here comes the twist: He followed this comment by saying that the feeling he got in the lab reminded him of some of the things that he liked to do, such as having dinner with his wife in a nicely lit restaurant with its pleasant ambience. He relished the romance of it, and he described what he felt to be one of "the little things" in life that he realized wasn't so little. He strongly felt that his romance with life included many little pleasures. Dinner with his wife in a tranquil restaurant, especially with soft jazz playing, qualified as an example of this sort of romantic aspect of life. When asked whether such, in fact, actually qualified as this kind of romantic experience, he answered:

> Yes, definitely, big time. I like that kind of environment in a nice restaurant. It gives me a good feeling. When I'm like that, I feel everything's good with the world. My wife is beautiful and I love her, and I know that she loves me. The music is playing, we're drinking wine, and we never run out of things to say to one another. I love to hear her talk, and she says that she finds what I say endlessly interesting. *Imagine that! She says that what I say is "endlessly interesting." She used those words. I can't get over it!*

Of course, I instantly recognized that this was the exact phrase Dennis used to describe the good feeling he got in the lab. Apparently, when he was there everything was good with the world, and thus he felt fine, accepted, loved and loving, endlessly interesting, and even romantic. *Imagine that!* When gazing at corpses in various states of dissection, this man felt romantic.

That's what it boiled down to.

This is also the irony. Here was a man who enjoyed feeling he had it all: He was conscientious, did all his work, married the woman he fell in love with, and had a sense that when you are responsible in life, everything will work out. This bit of his philosophy was truly the wellspring of his romantic sense of life. Do it right and everything will be fine. But then, there he was in a position in the hospital in which no matter how responsible he was, or wanted to be, he was still seen by his chief of service as someone who perhaps could not be trusted with important assignments. Dennis felt that given who he believed he was, given his stature, this didn't jibe with how he was being treated. It just was not the natural order of things.

### Describing the Symptom

Dennis described his symptom in detail. It would begin when he felt isolated, or after he was feeling shy, or withdrawn, or underutilized at the hospital. It would first start with an increase in tension. In other words, he knew that something was wrong when he would begin feeling insecure and uncomfortable. Only then would the idea of viewing corpses enter his mind. "If I could just see one corpse, my discomfort would disappear. I just knew it."

Then, when he could not immediately follow through on this urge, the urge itself would climb, and he would also feel a strong compulsion to go and do it. That is, he could barely wait for the day to be over so that he could scoot over to the lab and begin his gazing. At the end of his shift, and with great anticipation, he could actually rush over to the lab and, as soon as he saw the bodies, he would begin to relax. His tension would decline, and he would feel better.

This is when Dennis would spend undue amounts of time at the lab talking with the personnel about autopsies, techniques, and reasons for the deaths of the persons whose bodies were being worked on. Instead of coming home at a decent hour, he'd be perennially late. It was why his wife thought that he was being overworked. When she originally mentioned it to him he knew that the opposite was true. But he couldn't tell her the real reason.

It was all most bizarre and Dennis knew it. He also knew that the feeling of calm he got was exactly opposite the feeling that he would experience working in the department in which his chief was the absolute law. There he felt anxious and awful.

### The Symptom Code

Each element of the symptom code could now be applied to Dennis's symptom:

One: *The wish* that was thwarted or blocked was his desire to be valued as a physician. This was a direct wish, but it fueled another direct wish that was, obviously, for the death of his chief. He felt that he could only be valued if his chief was no longer in charge. Thus, the latter wish produced a symptom that reduced his tension. This was so because he wished that one of those corpses was his chief's.

Two: The sense that he was considered second-rate, and therefore not valued, made him *angry*.

Three: *The who* that he was angry toward, and about whom the anger was suppressed (or repressed), so that even he didn't know it was there, was this departmental chief.

### *Meaning of the Symptom*

Dennis was so angry with his chief that he was asking for that person's death. The main point is that the urge to continue viewing corpses was a repeated attempt to see his chief as one of those bodies (or all of them). He would always feel better gazing at corpses because, in a symbolic way, each time he looked at one it represented seeing the dead chief,

### To Do—*in Front of* the Line

Point Four: *the to do* was to have Dennis not shy away from his chief. Rather, *the to do* here was to be able to talk to the chief. Fortunately, this did occur and, again fortunately, the chief responded favorably so that a new and helpful attitude was forged between them.

*The one, two, three* of symptom-cure required knowing:

(1)   what *the wish* was
(2)   that the physician was *angry*
(3)   and that he was angry at his chief: *the who*.

The important point is that this physician was able to step *in front of the line* and articulate his discomforts. His symptom then quickly disappeared into thin air. Going to work each day began to give him a good feeling, so that his work gradually became one of those examples of the romance of life.

Finally, his urge to gaze at the dead was, itself, dead.

# CHAPTER EIGHT

# A Case of Body-delusion

*Holes All over My Body*

An elder gentleman awakens one morning and thinks that there are holes all over his body.

### *What Happened*

Charley, a man of eighty, awoke one morning and felt depressed, He found it emotionally difficult to get out of bed. When he finally forced himself to get up, he felt queasiness in his stomach. At eighty he was still a working-man, and although he had never before missed even a day of work, he nevertheless decided he just couldn't make it now.

Once out of bed, Charley felt that he had holes all over his body: holes that you could see through. This frightened him since he believed that if anyone had holes in his or her body he or she would die. His worry was shared by his seventy-five-year-old common-law wife whom he had lived with since his previous wife had died, about five years earlier.

A few days later, as the depressive feelings and the holes' symptom persisted, Charley also found that he was impotent. In addition, despite the fact that he and his wife were accustomed to a pretty active sexual life (age notwithstanding), he said that he now had no sexual interest whatsoever.

The entire emotional picture of what he called "the blues," including his delusion of holes in his body, his impotence, and his queasy-stomach, developed into a full-blown depression. When asked about the holes, he exclaimed, "You can see through them! They're all over my body!"

### Using the Symptom Code

Based upon our symptom code of *one (the wish), two (the anger),* and *three (the who),* we could guess that Charley:

(1) had his *wish* blocked

(2) got *angry* about it

(3) and didn't realize that he was angry at someone in particular: *a who.*

Charley reported that he had two sons. The older, at fifty, was a highly successful attorney, and the younger one, forty-three, was a struggling actor. As it turned out, this man had called his older son because, following a conversation with the younger one, the father realized that this younger son needed a loan. The father asked his successful-attorney son for this loan that he, the father, fully intended to repay on behalf of the younger-actor son. The older son was in a meeting, and although he took his father's call he dismissed it and abruptly ended the conversation.

It was the next day that our gentleman-elder awoke with his feelings of depression and holes.

### *Charley's Story Surrounding the Symptom of the Holes and His Depression*

It is true that the real problem here was Charley's symptom of holes and the issue of his sudden-onset depression. Yet, there was more to this eighty-year-old's life than met the eye. He said that he had never mentioned what he was going to say to anyone before, but now he had to get it off his chest. He related that throughout his life, from time to time, women would tell him that he is good-looking, and they were attracted to him. Also, from time to time, he would indulge in extramarital affairs, especially since his previous wife had been ill for many years before she died.

Even though he cared for her in all ways, he nevertheless couldn't remain celibate and therefore didn't resist sexual temptation.

But that was incidental. The real story was about a woman that worked as a secretary in the office of the firm, in the needles-trade industry, in which Charley was employed for the past forty years. She, too, had been employed there a long time, almost twenty years. She was eight years his senior, and in all the time they worked together he had a huge crush on her. He explained to me that he loved her but that she was married and would never contemplate any kind of extramarital affair. Instead, he befriended her and, in fact, they actually became good friends. He said that she knew he loved her but disregarded this and never gave him any reason to feel that she was flirting.

After his wife died, Charley met the woman with whom he had shared his life for the most-recent five years. He loved this woman and, for the second time, he again said that they had a good sexual relationship and were good companions. Yet, he carried a longing for the different woman he worked with. He explained that for the past year she, who at this time was approaching ninety, had become ill and was bedridden. Her husband had died some years earlier, but she still did not agree to have any contact other than one of friendship. However, since she was ill and since she had no children, she was really alone.

This was his chance to do something for her, not only because he felt it would endear him, but also because he really wanted to help. He would shop and cook for her and, in the early evening, he would sit by her bedside before returning home. According to Charley, his present wife never had a clue about this alternative-life of his, and he would unfailingly be home by 7:30 each evening for supper.

Thus, Charley would spend about one hour a day, Mondays through Fridays, at the bedside of this coworker for whom he pined. On the weekends, he would steal away for an hour or so and do the same thing: shop for her and sit with her. The heartbreak, however, was in his request to hug and kiss her, for which he repeatedly asked and which she invariably refused. So he settled for simply talking and just being with her. But given his experience with other women in his life, he no longer could understand this rejection.

With respect to his sense of pride, with the fact of his stellar work-ethic as well as the esteem in which he was held at the office, with regard to his joy in his sons as well as the fact that his common-law wife loved him (and, as noted, he loved her), all of this comprised a catalog of good things that counteracted his disappointment based upon the yearning that he had for the other woman and the deprivation (as well as rejection) that he felt about it.

But then something happened that did, in fact, depress him and that in turn generated a host of psychological/emotional symptoms, not the least of which was his impotence and, of course, his depression and sense that there were holes all over his body. During this period Charley was even able to visit with his woman-friend, although he generated enough energy to arrange for a neighbor of hers to look in.

"The something" that happened to Charley to cause such an array of symptoms seems most likely to have been directly related to the phone call that he made to his older son and the effect it had on him.

### Describing the Symptom

Charley was slowed down by his depression. He lost his appetite, and his sleeping was disturbed. He would sleep restlessly, and he would awaken during the night always feeling badly. He more or less lost interest in everything around him. He would also obsess about the holes in his body, and he would repeat the words *hole* or *holes* many, many times. He would look down at his stomach, look up at his wife, and only say, "Holes." She reported that he never again mentioned his older son, but he brooded about the younger one.

## The Symptom Code

The symptom code was applied in the following way:

One: *The wish* Charley had, to help his younger son, was thwarted, and he was not able to face the humiliation that he felt about the phone call with his older son. His *wish* was an indirect one since he couldn't face either son. It was a wish to avoid both of them. Because of the avoidant nature of the wish, his symptom produced an increase in tension.

Two: Being summarily dismissed by his older son humiliated him, and this humiliation disguised his *anger* at this older son. Thus, he could only feel the humiliation but not the anger. *He suppressed the anger.*

Three: The depression–culprit here, of course, was the older, successful-attorney son. He was clearly *the who.*

## Meaning of the Symptom

It became obvious that the anger Charley suppressed was originally directed toward his older son. In addition to making him angry, the humiliation that he felt at being dismissed by this son joined forces with the rejection he was feeling from his secret, wished-for woman. Together, these circumstances made him feel inferior, inadequate, small, unworthy, rejected, and not whole.

The keys to the holes' symptom thus begins to be revealed.

The point is that the holes' symptom is a disguise about *the original wish*. What was his original wish? Apparently, it was for his older son to grant him a loan and then later to repay it. As such, a successful realization of this wish would make our elder gentleman feel good in contrast to feeling depressed and bad. It would make him feel adequate, not inadequate or impotent, and it would make him feel *whole* and not *with holes*.

Yes, the wordplay describes what happened. Charley wanted to be "whole"—complete—successfully helping his younger son. But his older son made him feel "un-whole," *so he began to see holes in his body*. This substitution of "hole" for "whole" represents his symptom of un-wholeness or depression; but underneath it all, and originally, the entire problem was that his wish was always to be adequate: "whole."

Due to the unfortunate incident with his older son, in which he was humiliated, he wound up feeling quite inadequate: *holey*. The holes meant inadequacy. His wish was transformed into an avoidant one not to see his sons.

Therefore being depressed, feeling impotent or inadequate, and seeing holes in his body related to his suppressed anger toward *a who:* his older son. A direct result of feeling humiliated by this son created a situation whereby the elder Charley could not face his anger, and so he suppressed or repressed it. What resulted was a body-delusion of holes, a symbol of un-wholeness.

## To Do: *In Front of* the Line

Finally, Point Four of the symptom code, *the to do,* or *the-in-front-of-the-line* activity, involved a request to hold a joint meeting between father and son. The meeting was held, and his son apologized, explaining that he was at a meeting and could not talk, and didn't even realize that he had ended the conversation with his father so abruptly. The explanation was accepted, and Charley's anger quickly dissolved.

*The one, two, three* of symptom-cure required knowing:

(1)  what *the wish* was

(2)  that Charley was *angry*

(3)  and that he was angry at *a who:* his older son.

Calm was restored to this family. Charley gladly got his loan, and in short order all his symptoms disappeared—including depression, impotence, the queasy-stomach, the unwelcome-sleep disturbances, and absence of appetite. He really did feel better, both because the good relationship with his son was restored and, of course, because his original wish to be whole was realized. This meant that his pride was restored and that he could continue with his life: going to work, sharing feelings with his wife, speaking to his sons, and continuing the care for his woman–friend, who would never yield to him in the way he wanted, as noted, even as widowed and ill. Despite his unfulfilled yearning for "the other woman," this strong, proud, eighty-year-old gent carried on as usual.

There were no longer holes in his body.

# CHAPTER NINE

# A Case of Obsession

*Thinking about Death*

A late-middle-aged woman obsesses about death, and she begins asking everyone the same question: *Do you think about it, too?*

## *What Happened*

Carol, a woman in her mid-sixties, who had a history of medical complaints, aches and pains, and worries of illnesses, was repeatedly diagnosed over the years as both histrionic and hypochondriacal (always thinking that she had some illness). In spite of her complaints she was always given a clean bill of health.

Carol had been married to a man who was more than twenty years her senior and who had died several years earlier. When her husband passed, her frantic reactions and complaints of worry about having a variety of illnesses increased. The sole exception to her anxious condition regarding her health was seen when she went to business.

Carol's husband, along with his partner, owned a physical-therapy practice. When her husband died, she took over his share as partner and became its administrator while the business partner conducted the actual clinical practice.

Whenever Carol worked in the practice, she was happy and never complained of anything. This work gave her an overwhelming sense of well-being and a feeling of power. She only became obsessed with death sometime after both she and the business partner agreed that they would need to close down the enterprise because the patient-clientele had decreased significantly.

Carol had two daughters that were most attentive to her. They indulged all her medical concerns. They chauffeured her here and there, and with them she was passive and dependent: even childlike.

### Using the Symptom Code

Based on our symptom code of *one (the wish), two (the anger),* and *three (the who),* we would guess that Carol:

(1) had her *wish* blocked

(2) got *angry* about it

(3) and didn't know that she was angry at someone in particular: *a who.*

At first, Carol was upset and depressed over the loss of her business and, in fact, she was unsure about why the business failed in the first place. She stated that her feeling of depression was always accompanied by some vague sense of dread, that there was something wrong. At some stage, and quite by accident, she met a former patient of the physical-therapy practice who told her that he was still a patient of her former partner in the partner's current private practice.

Carol then began an investigation to discover that her old partner had been poaching patients, and that this thievery had been ongoing since her husband's death. Yet, after discovering this subterfuge, rather than becoming consciously angry, this woman began to feel terrible, and it was then that she began to obsess about death.

### Carol's Story Surrounding the Symptom of Death-obsession

A neighbor whose apartment was directly below Carol began complaining that Carol was flooding her apartment. Water was damaging her bathroom ceiling and the plaster was peeling. After the third such incident, the neighbor called one of the woman's daughters and described the situation. She indicated that each time the ceiling was damaged she had to wait until it dried before anyone could repair and paint. She also indicated that Carol always paid for the damage and repair, but obviously something was wrong since it kept happening. The neighbor further indicated that she thought the daughter's mother was constantly taking baths, that she could hear the water running sometimes two or three times a day, and had begun anticipating that her bathroom ceiling could once again be flooded at any time.

When confronted with this complaint, our worried, death-obsessed subject readily confessed that she often bathed since she only felt reasonably OK when sitting in a bathtub filled with very hot water. She said that the hot-bath was relieving and that it gave her a sense of safety and security to feel not only warm, but very warm. She said she knew it was abnormal to want to feel so warm all the time and added that it was obvious to her that it was about needing her husband back: The hot-baths made her feel protected. In addition, she stated that along with feeling good about the baths, she also felt bad about them since whenever she stepped out of the tub after having soaked for long periods of time, her skin was wrinkly, and she hated that as well.

Needless to say, she was informed that she filled the bath too high. Normally, the excess water would have left through the overflow drain. But for whatever reasons the overflow-drain did not do the job. The overflowing water damaged the bathroom ceiling below. This explanation made all the difference, and the problem was cleared up. But the hot-baths she was taking continued for a much longer period of time.

She further added that when she was out and about, she felt distant, remote, and almost cold. That made her feel vulnerable and exposed and she hated it, and that was the reason she gave for needing to feel warm all the time. Of course, this kind of feeling that she had of being cold and distant correlated with the onset of her obsession in repeatedly asking people: Do you think about it [death], too?"

### Describing the Symptom

*Do you think about it, too?*

This is what she began asking everyone she met. She couldn't stop thinking about her life and, several times a day, she would obsess over her death. In addition, she would talk about her husband's death. She worried about the deaths of her daughters as well. The only person whom she never seemed to include in these death fears—and this seemed mighty suspicious as well as clearly conspicuous—was her former partner.

### The Symptom Code

The symptom code now could be applied to each element of her story.

One: Her *wish* was thwarted because in place of needing to be empowered in her business, she wound up feeling disempowered, like a failure. Her wish was an avoidant one since she was afraid to confront her partner. She was furious with him but really, due to her fear, wanted to avoid him. Thus, her avoidant or indirect *wish* produced *a symptom*—a death-obsession—which increased her tension.

Two: Of course, she became *angry* about this but, at first, refused to direct the blame to any specific *who*, so she repressed this anger.

Three: *The who* was her partner, who was really the one that she well knew was the culprit but could not acknowledge as the culprit. He was responsible for the demise of her business: its death.

## Meaning of the Symptom

Carol's obsession with death really began after her husband died. In this sense, her husband was the original *who.* This is so because, in spite of her love for him, she was also quite dependent upon him and, therefore, when he died this woman felt profoundly abandoned and, of course, angry about the abandonment. The point is that abandonment feelings will usually generate anger at the person who is gone: even despite the fact that the departed may have been loved.

So it was in this case. When her husband died, Carol began having flashes of fears of death. Psychologically speaking, she was most angry at him for leaving her so that her fear of death also meant that under it, all this obsessive fear-of-death symptom, was a reflection of even her wish for him to die. This dependent woman was so angry about her abandonment that she herself even wanted to die. Her anger covered everyone, including herself. Basically, however, her obsession, or fear of death, was covering her anger toward the original *who,* her husband. Death or no death, love or no love: He left her!

But that was the past. In the present, her partner's double-dealing was too much for her even to think about. Rather than being directly furious with him, her reaction to his thievery was to be anxious, to despair, and, essentially, to feel entirely helpless and disempowered. The absence of any obvious anger toward this partner was a sure sign this woman had suppressed (repressed) rage toward him.

At this stage, her death-obsession became practically phobic. That is, she became extremely fearful of death. Of course her deep-down wish (about which she was not conscious), was in this former partner's death. But because she so desperately needed to avoid the pain of her defeat, she also needed not to face her anger toward this partner: *this who.*

Her mantra then, referring to her obsession with death, and which she posed to just about anyone she knew—*Do you think about it, too?*—was a wish for the partner's death, and even her own. She was in great despair and unwilling to confront her real feeling, her anger, so that even the thought of fear of her own death may have been easier to manage emotionally.

### To Do—*in Front of* the Line

Finally, Point Four of our symptom code is *the to do.* Doing something is *an in-front-of-the-line* activity, which in this case would be to encourage Carol to engage in conversation about her situation, to the point of reviewing her feelings toward her former partner. This was accomplished, and after a while she began saying that she was "upset" and "very dissatisfied" about what happened to the business. Naturally, these expressions of *upset* and *dissatisfied* are code words for *anger.*

When Carol began to express her upset and dissatisfaction orally, everyone noticed that her mantra of *Do you think about it, too?* was being asked less frequently. After a while, Carol's anger became less distasteful to her, and she began expressing it more directly. She began actively talking about her partner's thievery.

One day, in an independent act that was quite unlike her, Carol phoned her lawyer. This was her first *in-front-of-the-line* "doing" act. She wanted to see if anything could be done to gain some justice regarding the partner's theft of her business.

*The one, two, three* of symptom-cure required knowing:

(1)  what *the wish* was
(2)  that Carol was *angry*
(3)  and that she was angry at her former partner: *the who.*

Once she became more fully aware of the extent of her anger toward her former partner, and after she phoned her lawyer to lay out the bare-bones of her problem, only then did she report the final relief from her death-obsession. She said, "It was like something being lifted."

She was also not as interested in her usual hot-baths. It's not that she gave those up completely. But she reported that her needs were fewer. What that meant was that she was less in need of such consistent comfort that the hot-baths afforded.

To top it off, what she meant by "something lifted" was that she no longer had the urge to ask: *Do you think about it, too?*

The obsession with death was dealt its own death blow.

# PART THREE

# What Does the Symptom Really Mean?

# CHAPTER TEN

# The Symptom Is a Neurotic Way to Gratify the Original *Wish*

## The Wish *Connects to the Symptom*

Freud, the father of psychoanalysis, proposed many grand theories. A number of these are extraordinary, reflecting the ring of truth about the workings of the mind and about people's psychological and emotional lives. Along with some of his great discoveries, however, were others that turned out not to be useful or true. Nevertheless, Freud's discoveries about the workings of the mind—especially the unconscious mind—were fabulous, ingenious, and, practically speaking, highly useful.

One of Freud's greatest discoveries focused on the workings of emotional or *psychological symptoms.* His main discovery about symptoms concerns why they develop and what they mean.

Freud's first discovery about symptoms is that there is a connection between the symptom on the one hand and what the person who is suffering with the symptom wanted, or wished for, on the other. That is to say, Freud saw that there is a direct connection between the individual's original *wish* (what the person wanted) and the appearance of the symptom.

Then Freud got more specific about the matter of the wish and the symptom, and theorized that not only is there a connection between the original wish and the symptom but that, in fact, *the wish is the symptom* and *the symptom is the wish*. Freud said that if the wish were not met, a symptom would develop. He also discovered that when a person has a symptom it is really the wish itself but in a disguised form. Thus, any symptom is the translation of the individual's wish in this disguised or neurotic form.

### *Why Does* the Wish *Connect to* the Symptom?

The question is: Why should that be? That is, why should a wish connect to a symptom: always and without exception? Of course, Freud wondered exactly that. Why should it be that *the wish* translated into *the symptom?*

Freud's answer was astonishing, a truly great insight and discovery. What he says is that, in the person's mind or psyche, *no wish will ever be denied.* That is the key. No wish will be denied! Freud knew, of course, that in reality people hardly ever get their wishes met exactly when or how they want. Therefore, even when in reality the wish is blocked, the psyche of the person does not permit this kind of disappointment to win the day.

How it works in the psyche is this: Even in the face of *a blocked wish,* the presence of a symptom will nevertheless represent the wish as fully gratified—but in the disguised form of, and as, the symptom.

*The symptom is the wish fully gratified, even though, at first glance, it certainly doesn't look that way.*

But how does this happen? What connects the wish and the symptom? This is the question that Freud never really answers. He got the connection between the wish and the symptom, but he didn't get the mechanism that tied them together and made the entire process unshakable. This unshakable process, this unmistakable *connection* between *the wish* and *the symptom,* this hardcore principle of how a person's psychological life works, is that the symptom will always be a symbol of the wish.

Again, the question remains: What is it that connects the wish and the symptom? What is this mysterious, powerful mechanism that makes it all work: for every person?

### *How* the Wish *Is Translated into* the Symptom

A story can be used to express how the wish eventually becomes gratified *through* the symptom, and *as* the symptom. This little story goes like this:

A person has a wish blocked. Therefore, this person feels disappointed since he or she can't have what is wanted. As is always the case, anger is generated toward the person—*the who*—responsible for thwarting the wish. The reason anger is always generated into feelings of helplessness or disempowerment or disappointment is that under such a state of lack of power anger is frequently the only way to regain power. But the anger also often cannot be expressed directly to *the who*—the person responsible for the blocked wish and resulting disappointment. In this sense, the anger has only one place to go, and that is inward: into the psyche or unconscious mind.

Here is the short story of the anger and the blocked wish:

The anger says to the wish: "I'm going into the subconscious mind so that I won't even realize that I'm angry at this person, this *who* that won't give me what I want. I have my reason for not being able to let this *who* know that I'm angry. So I really have to hide my anger from that person, that *who*—and even conceal my anger from myself."

The wish answers: "I'd like to go, too, since then I can get what I want."

So the anger says: "Hop on!"

The wish hops on the back of the anger and down they go, deep into the subconscious, and even deeper still into the unconscious mind right into the center of the person's psyche.

Then, deep in the unconscious mind, *the anger* and *the wish* fuel the person's unconscious furnace. The anger continues to stoke the furnace while the wish, which is now in the furnace, is transformed into the smoke that is rising in the chimney.

The base of this chimney starts in the furnace of the deepest unconscious part of the mind/psyche. As the smoke (the transformed *wish)* rises up the psychic chimney, it passes into the subconscious level of the mind, then into the almost-conscious level, and finally pours out of the chimney into the person's fully conscious life. But now the wish exists as smoke in the form of a symptom and not in the form of the original wish that took the ride with the anger in the first place.

Further, as long as the anger toward *the who* remains out of the person's awareness—that is, it remains in the deepest unconscious mind—*the symptom will also remain as a symptom.* Another way of saying this would be to get back to our story and propose that so long as the anger keeps stoking the furnace—that is, remains unconscious—the wish will remain in the form of a symptom: even forever.

It is only when the anger toward *the who* becomes conscious that the symptom can disappear. In other words, when the anger toward *the who* comes out of the unconscious mind and into consciousness so that the person is aware of the anger as well as of the corresponding *who* toward whom the anger is directed, only then will the smoke disappear.

*No more anger in the unconscious mind means no more symptom.*

The person that knows about his or her own anger but still cannot confront *the who* will not have a symptom. Yet if there does, in fact, remain some little bit of the symptom, it will be just that: a residue, weak and ineffective, and, in a matter of a short period of time, it would be erased altogether. The erasure of the symptom is more firmly accomplished when the person gets in front of *the line,* in a doing-place, and engages in some activity that connects the original difficulty (the blocked wish) with *the who.*

## RULES ABOUT ANGER AND SYMPTOMS

### Rule 1

Where there is a symptom, not only will there be suppressed anger along with the suppressed wish, there *must* be suppressed anger along with the suppressed wish.

### Rule 2

Where there is suppressed anger along with the suppressed wish, not only will there be a symptom, there *must* be a symptom.

### Rule 3

Where there is no symptom, not only will there not be suppressed anger, and not only will there not be a suppressed wish, there *cannot* be suppressed anger or a suppressed wish.

### Rule 4

Where there is no suppressed anger and no suppressed wish, not only will there not be a symptom, there *cannot* be a symptom.

Thus, when the anger is made conscious, and especially toward the intended *who,* then in all likelihood the symptom will collapse. In such a case, the psychic furnace closes down. No furnace and no smoke equals no suppressed anger and no symptom.

Now this story about the wish-symptom connection also gives us a chance to create rules or hard-core truths about suppressed-and-conscious anger, and also about the presence or absence of a symptom.

The missing piece between wishes and symptoms is revealed to be the manner in which the person manages his or her anger. Does the person realize that (a) he or she is experiencing anger and (b) that the anger is about someone specific, *a who?* Or is the anger toward *the who* suppressed and hidden in the unconscious mind? If the anger toward *the who* remains conscious, then: no symptom. If the anger toward *the who* is suppressed and out of consciousness, then: yes, symptom.

# CHAPTER ELEVEN

# Inaccessible Symptoms

*Those that Resist the Cure and Why*

In part 2 of this book, a series of examples was presented that considered symptoms that could be cured by the use of our symptom code alone. That is to say, these symptoms could readily be understood, attacked, and cured without the use of any medication.

In this part of the book, a series of symptoms will be presented that resists *the one, two, three, and four* of symptom-cure. These are symptoms that are so firmly dug in that no amount of psychotherapy could make any impact on the power of the symptom. Although there may be exceptions, the vast majority of such cases are practically immune to the talking-psychotherapy cure. In such cases, only medication that is specifically targeted to the person's problem, mood, and diagnosis will be able to neutralize or erase the symptom.

In contrast and as noted above, in the earlier chapters in part 2—the case of "bottles under the bed," the case of "the intrusive thought of strangling," the case of "gazing at corpses," the case of "body-delusions of holes," and the case of a woman's "death obsession"—each symptom was curable. That is, each was cured through the talking-psychotherapy method: by applying the symptom code of *the one, two, three, and four* of the symptom-cure.

There are thus only two categories of symptoms: (1) those that can be cured with the symptom code, which we can call *the accessible symptoms* and (2) those that cannot be cured solely with the symptom code, which we can call *the inaccessible symptoms.*

The Question Becomes . . .

> *What happens to a symptom that makes it an inaccessible one and, in addition, what is it that makes some other symptoms accessible, indeed curable, through the use of the talking method, by utilizing the symptom code?*

### What Is It about a Symptom that Makes It Accessible or Inaccessible?

To begin, we need to say that when a symptom is curable it is, indeed, accessible to the talking-cure. The symptom will be found, so to speak, residing in the person's psyche—in the domain of wishes; that is, in that part of the psyche devoted to wishes. The symptom will then be accessible to the talking-cure solely through the use of the symptom code of the above-referenced *one, two, three, and four* of the symptom-cure.

However when the symptom, because of specific reasons that will be pointed out below, is shifted in its location within the psyche, away from the arena of wishes, then the nature of the symptom, correspondingly, also shifts. Usually, and under circumstances of such a shift, it could be imagined that the symptom migrates in the person's psyche away from the part of the psyche that is devoted to wishes and into the realm of the psyche that is devoted to the housing of personality traits.

As such, the symptom is patched into the personality profile of the person and no longer becomes merely a symptom. Rather, in the arena of the personality traits, it now may be called *a symptom-trait*. It is still a symptom, but now, in the realm of traits, it has also acquired the cast of a personality trait. As a symptom-trait, the symptom is now ingrained—engraved as it were—within the personality as any other personality trait is engraved.

Therefore, the symptom is no longer only, or even, responding in a typical fashion to the individual's wishes.

*In the realm of personality traits, the symptom speaks a different language from the one it speaks when existing in the domain of wishes.*

Within the psyche, when the symptom migrates away from the domain of wishes and into the realm of personality traits, then the symptom code of the *one, two, three, and four* of symptom-cure cannot do its job. It can only do its job for symptoms that exist solely in the domain of wishes.

When the symptom migrates into the realm of personality traits, then the memory of *the who* becomes separated from the suppressed or repressed anger.

*As soon as the who becomes de-linked from the anger, then the symptom is no longer simply a substitute for the wish.*

As a personality trait now, the symptom becomes a personality print of the individual just as any other personality trait identifies or characterizes a person. As strictly a symptom that represents a wish (as in the curable-accessible symptoms), the symptom is isolated from the personality and sticks out from the rest of the personality like a sore thumb. Now, as a symptom-trait, the symptom is something else—usually so dominant that it swallows the personality whole and becomes the personality—not merely something alien that is separately sticking out of the personality.

### Why Would a Symptom Migrate toward the Realm of Traits and Away from the Domain of Wishes?

When anger is over the top so to speak, as in the person experiencing blistering anger, blind rage, or blazing fury, the psyche may need to eject such rage from the domain of wishes since in some individuals such great intensity of anger could threaten the very existence of the person's mind or of the psyche itself. The shift of the symptom toward the realm of traits, therefore, is a survival operation based upon the person's psyche needing to protect itself.

Thus when the anger is so thunderous and becomes suppressed, then with such an intensity of anger the life of the psyche could be threatened, particularly in a person who is fragile in the first place. The following shows the danger to the psyche that such anger could have.

---

**THERE ARE FOUR REASONS FOR THE PSYCHE TO EJECT A CERTAIN KIND OF ANGER**

(1) *The magnitude* of such an anger–emotion—the extent to which it radiates or covers the psyche— may be too great for the psyche to manage.

(2) *The intensity* of the anger may be too concentrated an intensity for the psyche, as in a cataclysmic blow.

(3) The anger may have *penetrated* or imploded too far into the psyche for the psyche to remain stable.

(4) *The duration* of such anger simply may have existed for too long a period of time.

---

Under such conditions, the symptom will be ejected from the psyche's domain of wishes and begin to migrate toward the realm of traits. These conditions exist when the nature of the anger has *a magnitude, intensity, penetration,* and *duration* that is far beyond any average experience of anger, especially in a person who can feel emotionally injured too easily.

In part 4, which follows, examples of such severe-inaccessible or resistive-symptoms will be presented. These cases respectively include a case of compulsive hoarding, a case of anorexia, a case of agoraphobia (fear of open spaces), a case of delusional self-incrimination (blaming oneself of crimes never committed), and, finally, a case of split-personality.

In such cases, the only way the symptom code can contribute to a cure of the symptom is with the additional contribution of a medication regimen.

# PART 4

# Symptoms that Need Medicine to Be Cured

# CHAPTER TWELVE

# A Case of Compulsive Hoarding

*Chaos*

A man fills his house from top to bottom with tools, used furniture, and wood.

## *The Problem*

Fifty-five-year-old Nicholas lived with his wife and daughter in a small two-bedroom house in a rural area. He had been injured at the machine-shop in which he worked and was now in retirement. He was a master craftsman and could build almost anything. The problem was that he never finished a thing he started so that the house would fill up with half-finished tables and chairs, bureaus, and materials of various other uncompleted projects.

In addition, Nicholas was a hoarder. He would collect pieces of wood, stray lumber of any sort, tools, and broken-down furniture. When the materials would begin to threaten all the space of the house, his wife would throw out whatever she felt was junk. Of course, this man would become furious whenever she did this. His answer would be to redouble his efforts and quickly replenish his treasure.

Eventually his wife couldn't keep up with it and, soon, not a single surface in the house was clear. At a certain point neither his wife nor his daughter could stop it, and the entire house began to fill up. Then it wasn't possible to walk through the house without clearing a path.

His daughter was unable to invite any friends to the house, and eventually, when Nicholas refused to seek help, his wife and daughter finally left. By the time they had decided to leave he had already created the second layer of materials that were stacked and piled onto the first layer.

The clutter was world-class: chairs on tables on top of more broken furniture and so on toward the ceiling.

This was an example of a psychotic picture: what's known as a mental breakdown or, simply, as craziness. It was, in the language of symptoms, an accelerated-compulsive need to collect, ultimately for the purpose of hoarding. What this hoarding really amounted to was a house full of junk.

### *Early History*

"It always felt good," Nicholas explained. He meant that even as a child he felt good about saving things. He reported that when he was quite young he never finished anything that he started. Nicholas was always called a procrastinator by his parents and teachers. He reported that as long as he could remember, his tension could always be cured when he found something that he could collect. Thus, it seems that his compulsive-symptom of collecting was lifelong; or, what is known as *a chronic problem.*

In this sense of his chronic problem, Nicholas's collecting became a personality inclination, or it took on the cast of a personality trait, quite early in his life. Therefore, the symptom became familiar, the way a personality trait is, and no longer was merely an alien aspect of his personality as a symptom would typically be. The early picture of Nicholas's childhood was also one in which his room was in a steadily chaotic state. It was cluttered, and apparently there was not much his parents could do about it.

The man was one of three children. He was twelve-years younger than the youngest of his two sisters. He claimed that he was under-supervised by his parents who, by the time he came along, were quite tired. His sisters were busy with their own social-lives, and he had little memory of them from childhood.

His memory of his mother was of a controlling woman who only wanted things her own way. He said he thought his father was weak and, overall, his memory of his father was vague.

Almost never completing any of his assignments, Nicholas eventually dropped out of high school in his senior year. He remembers being almost-always anxious about something or other, and he admitted feeling inferior to others his age all through his growing-up years.

Associated with his later serious-compulsive hoarding, and his obsessional sense of ruminating about it all the time, was what he did near the end of his last high-school year before dropping out. This *something* was terribly revealing about his personality and what it meant about his problem. Nicholas reported that he always wanted to know things, but due to the fact that he never did his homework he felt that he never learned anything. He meant that he literally felt that he didn't learn a single thing in high school. Yet, he wanted to know things and actually yearned to be able to do his work. But he was hopelessly unable to organize anything, and so everything was always scattered about him and, even more importantly, he was scattered within himself.

Obviously, Nicholas had some aspect of an attention-deficit disorder that is consistent with the inability to organize oneself and is characteristic of scatteredness. He said that he could not explain any of it to his parents even though he wanted to since he felt that he wouldn't know where to start or how to explain it all. He also believed that they were not that available and actually were too busy for this kind of analysis. Thus, he always felt at loose ends about things and could never even get his homework-assignments completely down on paper so as to know what to do even if, by chance, he would have been able to do it.

What did Nicholas do instead? He began spiriting home objects from his chemistry-lab class. It appears Nicholas had a need to know how things worked: how mixtures of things go into making something new. The problem was that he had not learned a thing in chemistry and was failing. Yet he was stealing chemicals and test tubes as well as the racks that the tubes sat in, and spiriting them into his room at home. He kept them hidden until his mother wasn't home. Then he filled a test tube with various chemicals and, based on his *wish* that he was, in fact, really knowledgeable about what he was doing, he heated the test tube containing the chemical mixtures over the stove in the kitchen. On the first try, the chemicals erupted out of the tube hitting the wall.

This result, stemming from not knowing something that he pretended to know, ended his short career in chemistry.

The drama of Nicholas's *wish* to be a scientist who knew what he was doing was based on his impoverished-knowledge base, for which he created a fantasy-springboard—at least for a moment or two—thus enabling him to feel knowledgeable. Of course it didn't work, and the test tubes and racks joined the other junk in his room to remain part of his growing collection of debris.

All it became was more material to hoard.

### What It All Meant

We know that Nicholas treated his tension by collecting and hoarding. In fact, he stated that the more he hoarded the more solid he felt. It is tempting to guess that because he felt so unfinished in his family, he mirrored this feeling by leaving everything he did unfinished. He indicated that when he was a child it seemed to him that no one ever talked to him. His answer for all of it: *I think I always wanted to fix something.*

It may be, with respect to what it all meant—meaning his collecting and hoarding—that Nicholas, underneath it all, always wanted to fix his situation; that is, *to fix his family.* Even more basic, he may have wanted *to fix himself* and felt it was necessary to take things into his own hands since no one was giving him any attention. Therefore, it is assumed that he was angry at the condition of his isolation and also that he felt it was hopeless to depend on others.

Nicholas's fixing-wish motivated him to collect and hoard tools and wood, and the mere act of doing so was important to him since, symbolically, it represented a time in the future when everything would be all right. Under such a condition, wherein everything was imagined as being already fixed, or about to be, he would not have to be so angry all the time. His symptom of collecting and hoarding always made him feel better—it lowered his tension—since he treated it all as though it represented a repair of his fractured-family situation and thereby neutralized his suppressed or repressed anger.

It was never necessary to complete anything since the collecting and hoarding already satisfied his *wish:* that is to say, his psychological aim was never really to build anything in the first place. Rather, it was all symbolic. To fix something or to complete the making of a piece of furniture, for example, was only to focus on the reality of the object: that furniture. His was not an issue of reality, however, since the materials for making the furniture only served psychological and emotional wishes, and they were not at all based upon really making a chair or table.

Nicholas had bigger plans than making a chair. He was collecting and hoarding as a way of repeatedly assuring himself that his family was, in fact, already fixed and complete, and also that he himself was fixed and complete. His direct *wish* of having everything fixed related to his feeling less-tense when he actually played out his symptom of collecting and hoarding.

Furthermore, it is significant to note that his hoarding was a replacement and symbol of knowledge: of knowing things. As long as he hoarded, it meant that the family was fixed and that he was fixed, primarily because it also meant knowledge. That was the basic symbol of hoarding—knowledge—the feeling that he, indeed, did know something.

### Anger and the Psyche

The collecting and the hoarding concerned Nicholas's unconscious *wish* to be fixed, and to be fixed also meant that he had knowledge: that he did learn something in spite of the fact that, in high school, he was absolutely sure that he had learned nothing.

But it was his unconscious anger that connected the symptom of collecting and hoarding to *the wish to be fixed*. It was his anger about his situation that, as a child, he couldn't face, and more so that he dared not know about. In this sense it may be that a great amount of anger was suppressed or repressed, and the nature of the anger may have been overwhelming, especially since his symptom developed when he was so young and didn't have the emotional resources to deal with the frustration: perhaps particularly with his possible sense of abandonment. This is to say he felt that no one in the family had time for him.

It would be a case wherein this sort of anger threatens the life of the psyche since the sense of neglect and the sense of emotional abandonment became so entrenched that his isolation was the fuel that kept generating his anger since it represented everything that he hated about his life.

Hypothetically due to this, Nicholas's symptom was ejected from the psyche and began to migrate toward the realm of personality traits. This kind of anger would have *a magnitude* that covers the psyche, *an intensity* that pulverizes it, a power of *penetrating* deeply into the psyche, and the force to sustain itself over time: *duration* even over a lifetime.

This was definitely a case in which the use of medication would be necessary, to enable a successful application of the symptom code so that the compulsive hoarding could be reconstituted into an original tension—namely, Nicholas's sense that he was broken and that he felt he was undereducated. In this, its raw form detached from the hoarding symptom, he could then possibly be able to talk about his inadequacy-concerns without having to act them out in the form of a symbolic-hoarding system.

# CHAPTER THIRTEEN

# A Case of Anorexia

*"Not Thin Enough!"*

A young woman's mantra is: *Not Thin Enough!*

### The Problem

Michele, twenty-eight-years old, was hospitalized following a suicide-attempt. She was found semiconscious in her garage. The engine of the family car was running with the car-windows and door to the garage shut. This suicide-attempt was considered serious and not merely a gesture for attention.

She was an anorectic woman, and this was her major symptom, having lasted over the preceding twelve years. Her mother indicated that Michele began fretting about food at age sixteen, and she began to worry about her weight—actually, first of all, more about how she looked and whether she was too fat. Then, gradually, Michele began pushing food away, and whenever she would be looking in a full-length mirror she would repeat to herself: *Not thin enough!*

From then on, from time to time, Michele seemed to be withdrawn and depressed. The anorexia, however, was her centerpiece symptom. Rather than showing itself only as an occasional symptom, the anorexia was consistently present, never letting up. It was as though the anorexia symptom was a force, actually a demon that had a powerful influence over her in the form of a constant urging to look at herself in the mirror. Invariably, when seeing her image, the final facet of the symptom would reveal itself; that is, Michele disappointingly always thought, again: *Not thin enough!*

It was also the case that Michele had developed amenorrhea. She had not menstruated for the eight months prior to her suicide-attempt.

### *Early History*

It became evident that Michele was dependent on her mother, but she was also impatient and somewhat negative with her mother. Yet, Michele talked everything over with her mother, including sexual intimacies. She desperately needed her mother's approval, but she was also frequently angry with her. Both her love and her anger, in large measure, were caused by this dependency. This sort of double-take is called *having ambivalent feelings*. It means *ambi-valent:* two forces coming from the same place and going in opposite directions.

Michele's relationship with her father was not good, and she never respected his opinion or sought him for advice. It was clear that her mother was the power of the household. Michele *and* her father went along with all decisions the mother made.

Michele had one sister who was ten-years younger and she had almost nothing to do with this younger sibling. She said that her life was so busy that she figured her mother would take care of things related to this sister. However, Michele did have a best friend with whom she shared all her secrets and everything else that was going on in her life. They had been friends since they were four-years old and, essentially, grew up together until they were twelve. They would have sleepovers, dinner at each other's homes, travel together, and did homework together since they were even in the same class.

Then the bomb!

At that age of twelve this friend made other friends. Michele became instantly despondent. She felt abandoned and said to me that she was "in shock." Suddenly, this best friend more or less disappeared. Michele felt disoriented. Her friend had been so important to her that she was left without knowing what to do or where to go. Yet before long, the shock was absorbed and life went on. However, Michele never forgot the catastrophic feeling she experienced.

Although she was always a finicky eater, at this point in her young life Michele had not yet become anorectic. What happened was that she became overly critical of her mother and of anything else that, according to her, warranted criticism. Ironically it was then, and in spite of her critical attitude toward her mother, that her only relationship remained solely with that of her mother.

### What It All Meant

This brings us to Michele's present dilemma. The pivotal event that led to her suicide-attempt concerned a man that she had met a year earlier, which was four-and-a-half months before the appearance of her amenorrhea. She had fallen in love with him. This man seemed to like her and told her that she was pretty. However he was direct, and he also told her that he would be honest, saying that she was "Nothing but skin and bones."

He told Michele he would like to have a relationship with her and that he could see that she was beautiful and bright; at the same time he couldn't or wouldn't plan anything serious with her because of her unusual underweight-appearance. She seriously considered reversing her entire pattern of eating and its effect of weight-loss because she wanted to please him. Yet whenever she looked in the large mirror, which occurred several times each day, she would see *Not thin enough!* and could not, in reality, change her ways.

In short order this love of her life, this direct-talking gentleman, was gone for good. Michele was devastated by his disappearance, but she kept getting thinner. Even though she wanted to look the way *he* wanted her to look, she couldn't do it. She could not resist the urge to be thinner. A few months later, and immediately before her suicide-attempt, she learned that this man had become engaged. It was then that she began verbalizing to herself: *Maybe suicide would work for me.*

The fractured relationships with this man whom she loved as well as with her preadolescent best friend must have created a well of anger in her, which she ultimately directed at herself. It contributed greatly to the kind of symptom—the anorexia—which became her personality-signature. Michele recalled and talked about the earlier experience with her young friend when she heard that the man she loved was getting married. She then felt, *It's happening again. I can't go through this.*

Even though the suicide-attempt was serious it was not her main symptom. This is due to the fact that no matter how serious this attempt was during its process it was still mostly under her voluntary control, and she could have changed her mind about the act as well as call for help almost whenever she wanted.

It was the anorexia that she couldn't control and, therefore, her actual symptom *was* the anorexia. True enough, the experience of feeling abandoned and rejected by this man, combined with the memory of her preadolescent friend that it reactivated, certainly contributed to her despondency and subsequent suicide-attempt. But the intent of suicide itself was an acute acting-out, whereas the anorexia ruled her life for the longest time and would continue to be the prevalent *symptom* of her life.

It was this symptom of anorexia that "swallowed her whole" and entirely took over her personality. It *became* her personality. Anyone who described her would identify her solely with the layperson's term: *the anorexic.* Everything in her life revolved around this symptom. As such, it would seem that the symptom of anorexia shifted from the arena of wishes in the psyche into the realm of the psyche devoted to the organization of personality traits.

### Anger and the Psyche

The anorectic symptom was really "saying" something specific. Like any symptom it had a symbolic meaning. In this case, looking in the mirror and seeing *Not thin enough!* really meant, *The anger is still there.* The point is that there is no reality-relation between getting thinner and thinner on the one hand and being less and less angry on the other. A person cannot rid herself or himself of suppressed or repressed anger toward *a who* by becoming thinner. A person can feel better when going from obese to normal weight, but getting thinner to erase anger toward *a who* is not in any way realistically connected.

Yet in her psyche, Michele made the symbolic connection between anger and thinness even though, as stated, in reality there is no such connection. Such a fantasy-connection is *a behind the line* connection—a connection made out of a sense of withdrawal—completely in relation to her inner needs. But again, it is not reality-related. In her unconscious mind this connection, at best, might be defined as an attempt on her part "to thin out" her anger. Why is this? It is because the anger may be directed at her mother—the likely *who.* The problem is the ambivalence; that is, she loves her mother but is also angry with her. Due to her dependence on her mother it becomes necessary to eliminate the anger: to thin it out. The extended problem is that it is forever *Not thin enough!* Again, the reality is that there is no connection between erasing anger and the extent of one's thinness.

This fantasy-connection between anger and thinness likely occurred since it is assumed that the anger toward the possible *who*—in this case, presumably, her mother—forced Michele's psyche to remove the symptom from the domain of wishes and into the realm of personality traits. This would have occurred by the psyche's mechanisms de-linking the memory of *the who* from the repressed anger. Thus, the memory of *the who* could be concealed from the person herself that suffered the symptom.

In this case, since the anger toward this *who* was so dangerous, the anorexia was then transformed from a symptom to *a symptom-trait*. The reason the psyche had for pushing out the symptom from the domain of wishes to the realm of personality-traits concerned the psyche's sense of threat to its viability and integrity. That is to say, the danger this anger posed may have been of great *magnitude* covering all of the psyche: of great *intensity*—quite muscular, deeply *penetrating* the psyche, and of long *duration*—the symptom existed for many years.

At bottom, the anorexia-symptom was a gratification of the direct wish to love her mother and not be angry; and so whenever Michele didn't eat, her tension would be relieved. Thus, her symptom—the assertion of the anorexia—always decreased her tension.

Without medication this symptom could not be resolved or cured, and the symptom code of *the one, two, three, and four* of symptom-cure would not address it effectively. Only with the proper medication could *Not thin enough!* be approached with the symptom code, and in a way that could help resolve the emotional and psychological issues that underlie the anorexia: re-linking repressed anger with *the who* toward whom the anger is intended, then making it all conscious. The *to do* activity related to the problem of the ambivalence, and anger toward her mother would need to be crystallized in a way that produced some actual confrontation with the problem.

# CHAPTER FOURTEEN

# A Case of Agoraphobia

### *"I'm Not Going to Work Today!"*

A woman restricts her travel so that eventually she can't even leave her bed.

### *The Problem*

"I'm not going to work today!" was the first hint that sixty-year-old Norma was developing an agoraphobic (fear of open spaces) symptom. For the past forty years she had been a bookkeeper in a manufacturing firm. As it turned out, the owner began an affair with her that lasted almost twenty years. In this respect, despite her rather modest salary she now owned a condominium as well as a luxury automobile that, ironically, she almost never used. Her closets were jammed with expensive, tailor-made clothing. She never cooked, and each evening she only dined at expensive restaurants. Norma lived on his expense account.

After awakening one morning Norma exclaimed, "I'm not going to work today!" By the end of the morning she said, "As a matter of fact, I'm not going to work period." In a short amount of time thereafter, she would not leave the lobby of her building. Then she couldn't leave her apartment. This downward spiral continued till she couldn't leave her bedroom. Then she couldn't leave the area round her bed and, finally, she wouldn't even leave her bed.

### Early History

Norma had never married. She lived with her bachelor-brother for a ten-year period prior to her bookkeeping job. At that time she was both emotionally and financially dependent on her brother. This was merely a continuation of her strong reliance on her mother, all during childhood, when she would not leave home much, preferring to stay with her mom as much as possible. Her father had abandoned the family early in Norma's life. She said that her brother was the adventurous one, whereas she always needed protection.

Norma claims things were generally uneventful in all her growing-up years. She went through school with good grades, always did her homework, and felt rewarded for her efforts. Yet she would stick close to home. She spent all vacations away with her mother and, at times, also with her brother. She never had an eating-problem, and for the greater part of her early adult life was of normal weight. She was a rather tall woman, standing five-feet-nine-inches, so whatever extra weight she ever might have she would carry well.

When Norma went to work as a bookkeeper at this manufacturing firm she was about twenty-years old. For her first two decades working there, the boss of the firm, with whom she eventually had the long affair, was apparently never in any way aggressive toward her.

## *Then It Happened*

When she turned forty, the office personnel with whom she worked threw her a real shindig that the boss attended. For his birthday gift to her, he gave a business check in the amount of five-thousand dollars. She was flabbergasted, and when she told one of her close friends on the job about it, the friend said, "Watch out! He's after you." Her response was, "Don't be silly."

But of course it wasn't silly. Immediately afterward they went to dinner, and then it all started—for the next two decades. Over these years, the boss showered her with gifts, cash and otherwise, and it was during this time that she saved some of the money, invested the rest, and grew quite affluent.

She also became royalty at the office as it was no secret that she was the favorite and could do whatever she wanted. Everyone deferred to her, and her opinion about others carried all the weight necessary for whatever result occurred. She was universally liked by all her coworkers because she always went to bat for them whenever necessary.

But when her boss reached his eightieth birthday, the roof, so-to-speak, caved in.

### *What It All Meant*

Norma said that her employer-lover was a married man who obviously could not commit to her and be a full presence in her life. "He always told me he wouldn't leave his family," she said, "and everyone in the office knew this was true." Yet, in spite of this, she was quite proud of her status at the office where everyone knew that she was the boss's special person. She actually said, "It felt like I was the queen." She felt protected.

Then, of course, came the inevitable—the catastrophe.

On his eightieth birthday the boss told her it was too much for him to continue managing two relationships, and he wanted her to retire from the office. Then he presented Norma a timetable for her proposed vanishing act.

This was the pivotal blow to Norma's psyche, to her ego, and to her sense of security, which began her descent into severe agoraphobia. It was an emotional blow of the most severe kind, especially to an exceptionally dependent person and, more, particularly since there was no preparation for it. Her boss-lover announced it to her abruptly.

Her favorite restaurant was an Italian bistro that she had frequented almost every night for years. Of course, she was everyone's favorite patron, and she dined on the most-expensive menu-items. Now, confined to her personal circumference, she would order from the restaurant and an employee would deliver whatever she wanted.

Her only pleasure now was in eating, and it seemed that she was using food to tranquilize the anger along with any anxiety that may have even suggested the presence of the anger. Given the absence of any remotely defined aerobic exercise, along with the consumption of greater and greater amounts of food, Norma began to put on weight. Within a period of six months she had gained 40 pounds to add to her already filled-out frame of 150 pounds. At 190 pounds she was obese.

### Anger and the Psyche

At first after the breakup, Norma complained of feeling upset, sad, and terribly disappointed, and said also that she noticed that she was feeling "a little angry at him." Actually, she was probably raging at him underneath, but she didn't know it or couldn't face it. Usually, such a dependent person will conceal even the slightest note of anger largely due to the hope that the wished-for person, on whom the dependency is based, will return.

Her underlying rage was, in turn, based on the bare fact that she was left feeling helpless and, of course, entirely without any power. Norma was essentially disempowered. Her wish was also completely blocked or thwarted—the wish of needing this man's constant presence and support, as well as the actual needing of her virtual fix—the royal treatment that she got at work.

In a sense not moving out of her bed was her absolute insistence, symbolic as it may have been, that he come and get her. Therefore, her wish to remain in bed was her way of magically getting him back. In fact, in an unconscious-symbolic way, staying in bed even meant that, indeed, he *was* back.

The difficulty here revolved round the nature of the anger and rage that Norma was suppressing. *The magnitude* of the rage must have been huge and surely threatened her psyche. *The intensity* of the implosion of this rage or fury, that is, the inner explosion of the fury or rage, also must have been great. Additionally, *the penetration* into the psyche of such rage was also powerful and, over time, the symptom seemed to be simply another example of her lifetime-dependency problem, a dependency of long *duration.*

In this case, the symptom became profoundly entrenched. This was practically a sure sign of a symptom that would endure—even last forever—if not for the use of some miraculous-medication intervention.

Given this kind of rage, and without the use of medication, her psyche would have no choice but to eject the symptom from the domain of wishes and send it toward the realm of personality traits. The point here is that whenever anyone referred to her, they said things such as "she can't leave her bed." In other words, Norma, was becoming identified by her symptom as a trait of her personality, which people, indeed, considered sick.

Over time, the agoraphobic-symptom was so severe that Norma hardly ever mentioned her boss-lover at all and only concentrated on her condition of refusing to leave the bed. She was behaving as though her anger and rage were de-linked from the memory of *the who* (her boss-lover) despite the fact that she, indeed, very much remembered him. Nevertheless in her unconscious mind this linkage, of her anger on the one hand and his image on the other, was breaking apart.

Here was an ironclad picture of *a symptom* swallowing the personality whole and then becoming the personality in the form of a symptom-trait. In such a case, only medication could reach the symptom and only then could Norma use the symptom code of *the one, two, three, and four* of symptom-cure.

The way it stood, however, was that her agoraphobic-symptom represented a deep pathology or sickness in the form of a severe *behind-the-line* withdrawal, and the symptom, as an expression of her insistence that her employer-lover return to her was, in turn, not to be. Yet her symptom decreased her tension since in her unconscious mind it meant that her lover was actually there, even if he weren't.

Eventually, her refusal to leave her bed led to other refusals: mostly with respect to a refusal to be medically treated. Then came a sudden loss of appetite before heart failure tragically ended her life.

# CHAPTER FIFTEEN

# A Case of Delusional Self-incrimination

*"No Writing!"*

A man refuses to write because he believes that he has committed a crime and, therefore, is afraid his writing would be his confession.

### *The Problem*

In his fifties, Mike was the top salesperson in a men's clothing shop. But he was plagued with an overwhelming problem. It was a major symptom even though it didn't prevent him from working. He was a charismatic and charming person, and would be able to create good feelings with his customers. When it came to writing sales-slips, however, he would need to ask another salesperson to write these sales-slips for him.

Mike simply couldn't or wouldn't write. "No writing!" he would exclaim.

He was intelligent and, in fact, could write well. But in practice, in reality, he just wouldn't put anything down in black and white, and there could be no circumstance he could imagine that would make him want to write. He actually would pay others a percentage of his commission to write-up sales-slips.

His wife was also unable to get him to write these slips, and she was becoming more and more annoyed over his anxiety about such behavior. This was her constant complaint to him for the more-than-fifteen years that they were together. As a matter of fact, all through their marriage he never committed himself to writing anything. She, of course, knew his reason.

The problem was that he would always be tense, either whenever he read in the daily newspaper or heard on the radio or television, any story about some crime that had been committed. This was the issue: crime! It didn't matter if the crime was committed three-thousand miles across the country. It would still bother him and make him feel that others would think he did it. Moreover, even he would confuse himself into believing that perhaps he did do it. He wasn't sure, but he thought—*maybe.*

This was the problem: A clear belief or delusion of self-blame or self-incrimination. It was a delusion and it defied logic. Even if he were confronted with the impossibility of his participation in a crime that took place five-minutes earlier across the continent, so that he could not have possibly been there, it did no good. Thus, the problem was not about logic. It was only what he felt that persuaded him. Of course, it was this lifelong-chronic problem of being afraid to confess a crime that had a tight grip on him.

This delusion was so well entrenched that it was considered to be a psychosis or a craziness —one that was isolated from the rest of his personality so that it did not make anything else about him seem crazy. Yet this delusional self-incrimination symptom of no-writing swallowed his entire personality. Anyone could identify him by the presence of his *symptom*.

### Early History

Memories of his childhood were sketchy. He was an only child with parents who were forever disciplining him. His mother believed in strict punishment for bad behavior. His father was similarly strict and was, according to Mike, always sarcastic. Otherwise his father was a nonpresence in the family, and as Mike described it, "My mother ran the show." He then said, "With my parents I could never get what I wanted.

Generally, he expressed negative feelings about his parents and was especially negative regarding his mother. Once, when his parents were in a traffic accident, his daydream was that if they had been killed he would be free.

Other than these, everything else about Mike's memories of his parents was vague. The main point it seems was that with respect to his early history Mike reported feeling isolated and deprived of understanding and love. In addition, he felt angry at one or both of them. Again, his mother would be the best guess as the person toward whom he felt the most anger: especially since he specified that it was she who usually made it impossible for him to get what he wanted.

As a young man growing up, Mike was always somewhat short for his age but always compact, muscular, and strong. He was athletic. The love of his life was handball, a game played against a wall in which a player hits the ball with the palm of the hand without letting the ball bounce more than once on the pavement or gym floor. The opposing player does the same till one of them either can't get to the ball to hit it back or misses it, or hits it in such a way that makes it bounce twice or more before striking the wall. Devotees play the game with a high-bouncing, small-and-hard black ball. It's the sort of game that can damage someone's hand if the person is unaccustomed to the stresses. Mike, however, had a most powerful and fleshy palm, and hitting the ball was not only not painful, it was pleasurable.

When discussing his early in-life experiences of handball, Mike remembered that whenever he hit the ball it relieved his tension. He never figured out why this was. In his psychotherapy session, it was suggested that whenever he hit the ball it meant that he was rejecting any accusation of wrongdoing for which the world (his mother?) was faulting him. Whenever he would miss the ball he simply hated it because it gave him a bad feeling—far worse than a simple error in a game could ever normally generate.

His obsession with handball continued into his adult life, and he almost lived for it.

### What It All Meant

In discussing his parents, his daydreams of their car-accident was a clue as to how he really felt. From a psychoanalytic point of view, his thinking that they may have died in the crash so that he could be free was actually his wish for their death. However, this wish was not particularly well-thought-out or a conscious wish; therefore it was mostly suppressed or repressed.

Mike's delusion about participating in every crime in existence also reveals that he really had already convicted himself of the most capital crime—that of murder—probably of his mother. Presumably, that's what he thought: that he murdered his mother. Thus, he refused to write since in his unconscious mind he is certain that the only reason he has not been punished is that he has not incriminated himself by confessing to this crime through the written word.

It should be noted that Mike's mother was eighty-five-years old and very much alive when he met with me. Yet in Mike's mind, due to his ostensible wish for her death, he was compelled more by his feelings and not at all by the reality of what he knew: that is, his mother, in fact, was alive.

### Anger and the Psyche

Interestingly, when discussing his parents he could not consciously feel any rage or even strong anger toward them. He did, however, admit to enjoying the feeling of freedom that he got when thinking that they might have been killed in the car accident.

The point is that Mike was avoiding a considerable burden of guilt regarding what he may have unconsciously considered to be his responsibility in the murder of his mother. This wish for the death of a parent was gratified in *the symptom* of no-writing, since the no-writing meant that the deed had already been accomplished; he had killed her. Thus his direct wish was to remain guilt-free. Therefore, he wouldn't write! His direct wish produced a no-writing condition and this no-writing reduced his tension. Whenever he is required to write but doesn't, he's really hitting that handball. In so doing, he avoids responsibility for confessing to murder—to matricide.

Therefore, it is likely that the anger toward his mother was so great that its *magnitude* radiated his entire psyche, its *intensity* was similarly overpowering to the psyche, *the penetration* of the rage went deeply into the psyche, and the lifelong duration of the symptom meant that his psyche felt it absolutely necessary to eject *the symptom* from the domain of *wishes* and into the realm of personality traits. In any event, it can be seen that his personality was swallowed whole by the symptom so that he was known as the guy who wouldn't write.

Due to his vagueness with respect to his childhood memories, the prediction would be that suppression or repression of anger had occurred early in his life and had since de-linked from the memory of *the who*. This de-linking of the anger from *the who*— perhaps his mother—made the symptom incurable without medication. Without such medication no amount of psychotherapy could ever touch this symptom. The truth is that this man was so *behind the line* in a psychological and emotional withdrawal that only medication could address the delusional belief on which the symptom code was based.

With medication, however, ultimately the symptom code could easily be used to help cure the symptom.

As a postscript, it should be noted that the difference in understanding the therapeutic approach to belief versus delusion is that belief can frequently be challenged by facts whereas facts can never challenge delusion. The only approach to delusion rests on an analysis of the person's *wish*.

# CHAPTER SIXTEEN

# A Case of Split-personality

*The Sexual Self, the Aggressive Self, and* the Self Self

A classic split-personality appears in which three *personas* inhabit one body. First is the host or so-called normal one. Second is the aggressive one. Third is the sexual one.

## *The Problem*

A person with a split-personality is someone who, in psychiatric language, is referred to as *a dissociative-identity disordered* (DID) individual. What this means is that the person's identity is dissociated or, in other words, parts of the person's personality are located in different compartments—each separated or dissociated from the other. These compartments are so separate that in this split-personality or dissociative-identity-disordered type, at rock bottom, three personas exist in one person or in one person's personality. Even when there are many more than three personas that show themselves, these are really sub-units of the basic three.

The three basic personas are:

(1) the so-called normal one, known as *the host*
(2) *the aggressive persona*
(3) and *the sexual persona.*

At one time or another, each of these three personality components gets, so to speak, to do its own special thing. In this sense each persona—other than the host (known as *alters* or *alter* personality)—develops its own memories, emotions, personality style, even handwriting. What is truly amazing is the way the whole thing works.

And the way it works is thus:

(1) the host personality—the so-called normal one (the self)—does not know of the existence of the other two
(2) each of the other two—the aggressive and the sexual— knows of the existence of one another, and also knows of the host.

Thus the host is the one in the dark: not aware of these other two personalities lurking within and not conscious of what these other personas do when they take over.

What are these things that the aggressive and sexual personas do? *The aggressive personality* will do aggressive things such as fight, act in a hostile manner, be belligerent, become argumentative, be scornful, be smoldering, and generally protest everything in sight. *The sexual persona* will do sexual things such as flirt, be seductive, be promiscuous, be exhibitionistic and/or voyeuristic, and so forth.

Such was the case with Joseph. He was thirty-five-years old and had been hospitalized for the second time in one year—each time for depression. And each time he was hospitalized his depression lifted. He worked as a handyman to clients whom his adoptive mother cared for in her capacity as a home-health aide. He would become uncomfortable talking about this arrangement: he confessed that when his adoptive mother was at work, he felt deprived of her presence.

At the hospital Joseph was caught sexually exhibiting himself. He had been exposing himself in the women's ward. He escaped being detected during his act of exposure, but later was found in his room donning female clothing. He also had a collection of female toiletries and cosmetics. When confronted with all of this evidence it was too late. He had already switched. (*Switching* is used to mean the transformation of one *persona* to another.)

Thus, to confront Joseph with the fact that he was wearing lipstick could not shake his bewilderment about how that had happened. He could not understand how all such female paraphernalia inserted itself in his room. Additionally, a diary was found in his room. The diary was a conversation between a man and a woman. The man explained that he felt good only when attacking others, whereas the woman explained that she only felt good when being exhibitionistic and showing her (his) penis while pulling up the leather skirt she (he) was wearing. The diary went on like that: one or two pages from him to her, and then one or two pages from her to him.

Again, Joseph denied knowing anything about the diary or of any other event that took place either by his aggressive persona or by his sexual one. Along with this denial he experienced a philosophy of nonviolence, even though others on the ward complained that, at times, he was physically threatening to them. This, too, he denied ever knowing about.

### Early History

Joseph's early history consisted of a most-overprotective relationship with his mother and an extreme dependence on her. She adopted him when he was three-years old and soon thereafter divorced her husband, retaining full custody of her new child.

She home-schooled him. It appeared that he may not have had any friends whatsoever. In fact, Joseph actually could not name a single friend from his childhood. The picture was of a lonely boy having limited contact with others and, more or less, having his adoptive mother as his only relationship.

Everything he remembered about his childhood involved his adoptive mother. He denied having any sexual feelings toward her; but he was evasive in his answers to such questions, making it clear that it was likely there was more here than met the eye.

However, there were intimations of a great deal of seductive behavior at home. In describing this history, Joseph causally mentioned that his mother, a well-endowed woman, would typically walk about the house in her bra. In addition, he mentioned (as noted) that she was a disciplinarian and would not tolerate any back talk. "No lip from me!" is how Joseph expressed it. In addition, bathroom doors were never locked, and even when either of them was showering or bathing, the other would sometimes walk in and out of the bathroom. These revelations reached a crescendo when he reported that in their cramped apartment there was only one bedroom and that they shared the bed.

## What It All Meant

During his adoptive mother's visits to Joseph in his current hospitalization, she was not appropriately dressed. She offered a garish display of her voluptuous figure, both with respect to her style of clothing and the colors. Everything she wore was skintight, obviously designed to display her figure to what she considered to be its best advantage.

This seductive, ostentatious display of herself was an example of the influence that she had on this man even when he was a child. Joseph stated: "I love her, man. She's beautiful and always was—in and out of clothes." It was crystal clear that his only real interest and focus was on her.

In professional-psychiatric circles, it is generally accepted that a split-personality can develop from recurring physical and/or sexual abuse. With respect to the sexual issue, sexual favors can be given for obedience or merely for commonplace compliance—for the appearance only of behavior that is permitted. As Joseph's history unfolded it was revealed that this adoptive mother seemed to have controlled and manipulated him his entire life with the promise of her love, her seduction, or whatever the sexual favor would have been. In his own admission, he depicted a kind of worship that he had for her.

Regardless, he was not physically abused. Rather, it seemed clear that *he was sexually controlled.* On the one hand, he wasn't permitted to be aggressive or angry. On the other, apparently he wasn't free to be sexual except with her permission.

## Anger and the Psyche

It is also reasonably clear that this man's fractured self could not have occurred in the absence of a strong-and-intense anger that was being suppressed. The point is that when someone is controlled, utterly dependent on the controlling person, and, on top of it, also loves the person—madly loves that person—then that someone is no longer in charge of his or her personality. He or she would almost necessarily, and for survival-reasons, have to do the bidding of the controlling person.

This is what seemed to have happened here with respect to Joseph's life-problems. His split-personality swallowed all of him. Thus, in order for him to have salvaged some normalcy, in his unconscious mind his psyche ingeniously created three personas to make up for the problems of his one personality.

What were these problems? They were rules he got from his adoptive mother not to have aggressive or sexual feelings—at least not without permission. He obeyed but still created personas with their own emotions for which he was not going to be responsible. One was aggressive and the other sexual.

In this way, the purpose of such a personality-fragmentation is to escape painful and/or embarrassing memories and to sneak around the rules so to speak. Like this, as the host, as the person who does not consciously know of the existence of the other two, he is free of their so-called evil impulses and deeds.

This man's wish was to be a whole person but also to possess completely his mother along with obeying her. He got his wish by obeying her insofar as he was able to trade his sex and aggression for her favors. Yet his direct wish to be one *whole* person was gratified by his three-part personality that always reduced his tension as he was then able to express all facets of his personality without worrying about it. In this way he could curry favor with her and still be one person, albeit fractured.

This kind of obedience and worship carried with it a tremendous undercurrent of anger since, in anyone's personality, great dependency breeds great anger.

Naturally, the anger would be deeply suppressed or repressed, and it would be the kind of anger or rage that affected the psyche pathologically. In the sense of such pathology the psyche, without question, must have ejected the fractured-persona of this man—his split-personality—out of the domain of wishes into the realm of personality traits. The fractured or split-nature of Joseph's personality became his norm so that now he could be identified as "a split": the main identifying trait of his personality.

The reason his psyche would have ejected his symptom out of the domain of wishes and into the realm of personality traits concerns the threat to the psyche due to *the magnitude* of his anger, the powerful *intensity* of his anger, the deep *penetration* of his anger, and the chronic-lifelong *duration* of the symptom.

Essentially, this man was spending his entire life *behind the line,* in withdrawal and in a swoon with his adoptive mother who herself was, and continued to be, quite disturbed.

There would be no chance for him to cure his split-symptom solely through the talking-cure, utilizing our symptom code. In this case, once again, medication would be required that, together with the use of the symptom code, could address some of the issues of his fragmented personality.

Thus, a new treatment-approach needed to be developed so that this man's personality-fracture could begin to congeal or heal. Then he could be whole. This would only occur if his anger toward *the who*—his mother—would become known to him—conscious. As it stood, his repressed anger and his memory of *the who* were obviously dislocated so that his symptom was now a hard-core symptom-trait.

# PART FIVE

# Summary of the
# Symptom Code

# CHAPTER SEVENTEEN

# Summary of the Symptom Code and All Its Phases

## PHASE 1: BEFORE THE SYMPTOM FORMS

1.  Pleasure is what we want, and wishing is the chief representative of pleasure. It all starts with trying to get wishes met so that we can have pleasures.

2.  When a wish is blocked, the person feels frustrated. In this sense, having pleasure is now postponed.

3.  The result of a blocked or thwarted wish (and its accompanying frustration) is that the person feels helpless or disempowered.

4.  The emotional reflex to disempowerment is to feel angry. Anger in itself is a pleasurable release of frustration. The anger-reaction is natural because when someone feels disempowered anger frequently becomes the only way to regain the power: that is,

to become reempowered. To become always reempowered is what we always want.

5.   But in many cases, for one reason or another, it is difficult to want to express the anger or even to know that you have it. So what people do is suppress or repress the anger: push it down and out of conscious awareness.

## PHASE 2: NOW THE SYMPTOM FORMS

6.   As a natural by-product of this repression of anger, emotional/psychological symptoms appear since the nature of anger is that it is an attack-emotion. When the anger is repressed (along with *the wish*) it attaches to the self. When it does that it therefore attacks the self. *The symptom becomes the result of the self-attack.*

7.   Freud discovered that, in the person's psyche, no wish would be denied. Thus, when in reality *a wish* is actually denied, nevertheless in the psyche that same wish becomes actualized in the form of the symptom and as the symptom. *It could be said that we love our symptoms—even those that are painful— since they are our wishes gratified though disguised.*

8.   Due to this process, of the anger being repressed and the symptom then representing the gratified wish, rules regarding anger and symptoms are formed that indicate:

As far as anger is concerned

and

As far as *the wish* is concerned—

a.  Where there is repressed anger along with the repressed wish, not only will there be a symptom, there *must* be a symptom; and,

b.  Where there is no repressed anger and no repressed wish, not only will there not be a symptom there *cannot* be a symptom.

As for a symptom:

a.  Where there is a symptom not only will there be repressed anger along with the repressed wish, there *must* be repressed anger along with a repressed wish; and,

b.  Where there is no symptom, not only will there not be repressed anger and not be a repressed wish, there *cannot* be repressed anger and there cannot be a repressed wish.

## The All-important *Who*

9.  The reaction of anger is always about a person, *a who*. The emotion cannot simply hang there as if suspended in midair. The anger seeks *the who*.

10. At times, when the other person is absent or for whatever reason is unavailable, or cannot be directly confronted, then the self becomes the target of the anger. The emotion of anger therefore still has a person to attach to: the self.

**PHASE 3: LIFTING OF THE SYMPTOM**

11. When the target of the anger—*the who*—is identified, and the anger toward this *who* becomes conscious, then the strength of the symptom is challenged and the symptom may instantly disappear.

12. The symptom will be challenged more decisively if, after *the who* is identified and the anger becomes un-repressed and thus conscious, the person becomes actively involved in *a to do* activity involving the original wish. This *doing* activity will strengthen the erasure of the symptom. *The doing* activity places the person in front of *the line:* in a reality-place and out from *behind the line;* that is, from withdrawal, where symptoms thrive.

**RESISTIVE SYMPTOMS**

13. When the symptom results from a major explosion inward (an implosion) of anger, so that *the magnitude, intensity, penetration,* and *chronicity* (lifelong symptom) of this anger maximally radiates the

psyche, then the symptom can only be overcome through the use of medication.

14. Otherwise, the symptom can be cured through *the one, two, three, and four* of our symptom code: by knowing *the wish, the anger,* and *the who,* and by implementing *the to do.*

# Index

(*Italic* numbers reference a term-definition.)

# About the Author

Spanning a 60-year career in the field of mental health, Dr. Henry Kellerman has held professional academic appointments in the psychology doctoral programs at several universities and clinical appointments at several mental hospitals. In addition, Dr. Kellerman was a Training Analyst and Senior Supervisor at the Postgraduate Center for Mental Health Psychoanalytic Institute.

Dr. Kellerman has published scores of papers in professional clinical and scientific journals, published 35 authored and edited books, and presented papers at local, regional, and national conferences. He has been in the private practice of psychotherapy since 1965. He holds Fellow status in the American Psychological Association, the American Group Psychotherapy Association, and the Academy of Psychoanalysis, and is a Diplomate in Clinical Psychology and in Psychoanalysis, of the American Board of Professional Psychology.

Dr. Kellerman's books published by The American Mental Health Foundation include: *Personality: How It Forms*; *Anatomy of Delusion*; *There's No Handle on My Door: Stories of Patients in Mental Hospitals*; *Psychotherapeutic Traction: Uncovering the Patient's Power-theme and Basic-wish*; and, *Group Psychotherapy and Personality: A Theoretical Model.*

*Academic credentials include: Master of Arts in experimental psychology, Master of Science in clinical psychology, doctoral degree (Ph.D.) in clinical psychology, and certificates in postdoctoral training both in individual psychoanalysis and psychoanalytic group psychotherapy.

CPSIA information can be obtained
at www.ICGtesting.com
Printed in the USA
FFHW022119281019
55841569-61709FF

9 781590 566053